Mastering the
Essay

Advanced Writing
& Historical Thinking Skills

AP* European History Edition

by Tony Maccarella

REVISED EDITION
Includes the Summer 2017 Course Revisions

Sherpa Learning is dedicated to helping high-achieving learners gain access to high-quality, skills-based instruction that is created, reviewed, and tested by teachers. To learn more about Sherpa Learning and our vision, or to learn about some of our upcoming projects, please visit us at **www.sherpalearning.com**.

Publisher/Editor: David Nazarian

Copy-Editor: Christine DeFranco

Cartographer: Sal Esposito

Cover Image: Il Duomo of Florence, © shutterstock.com/Luca Villanova

This edition has been revised to reflect changes that were made to the course and exam by the College Board® in the Summer of 2017.

* AP is a registered trademark of the College Board®, which was not involved in the production of, and does not endorse, this product.

ISBN 978-0-9905471-3-6

SHERPALEARNING
GUIDING YOU TO EVEN GREATER HEIGHTS

Printed in the United States of America.

10 9 8 7 6 5 4

This book is dedicated to my dad, who taught me the value of seeing things through to the end. Without him, this book would be just another dream.

Wish you were here to see it, Dad.

Brief Contents

Table of Contents

Table of Contents

Introduction

If you are like most AP European History students, you are concerned that you may not know enough facts to score well on the Multiple-Choice section of the exam, and you are probably not-just-a-little intimidated by the prospect of a brand new AP exam format that includes Short-Answer Questions and two thesis essays, one of which is the always-mysterious Document-Based Question (DBQ). You have, no doubt, heard that these essays are all hand-scored by unknown people in unknown places, each certain to apply his or her own standards of quality to the task. Since you have no way of controlling who scores your essays, or which standards they apply, you are relying on the Multiple-Choice Questions to carry your score. You're not about to take chances and just hope you and the mystery reader are on the same page. As a result, you are probably somewhat dismayed by the lack of review terms and multiple-choice practice questions in this book, and are wondering where you can buy a "real" AP prep book.

Fear not! *Mastering the Essay* is better than AP prep books because this book focuses on the often-neglected part of the exam—the part that *will* make or break your score—the essays. If the previous paragraph describes you, then the first thing you must learn is that most of your preconceptions about the essay section of the AP exam are absolutely false. The AP readers who score your essays are high school teachers and college professors—people not often known for their mysterious origins. Even less mysterious are the standards by which the essays are assessed. The College Board® (the organization that writes the AP exam) has created very clear guidelines for assessment, and the test-makers spend many hours training each reader to apply these standards accurately and consistently. In fact, your essay will almost certainly receive the same score regardless of which of the AP readers assesses it.

I am one of those AP readers, and I have written this book to help you, the AP European History student, learn the standards by which your essays will be scored. By learning what's needed for a top score, you will be better prepared to incorporate these things into your essays. Even the very-scary DBQ is scored according to these standards. Developing the necessary skills to succeed on the AP essays will not be an overnight task, but if you follow the step-by-step process detailed in the pages that follow, before you know it, you will be writing essays that regularly score at the top end of the AP European History rubrics.

As an added bonus to using *Mastering the Essay* instead of some run-of-the-mill AP prep book, the skills needed for writing great AP European History essays are the exact skills needed for writing great college-level history essays. Rather than wasting months preparing for a single day in May, spending time developing better writing skills with *MTE* is an investment in college success. So put the prep books back on the shelf—*Mastering the Essay* is the only "prep" you need to achieve the highest score on the AP European History exam and to write college-level thesis essays.

I have designed each unit to explain one particular part of the writing process. Each instructional section is accompanied by a set of practice exercises in the Exercise Workbook to assist in developing your skills. I set out to make this book useful to students in any AP European History class, no matter which specific topic is being studied. Each exercise set is divided into chronological practice questions that mirror the new AP Course Outline provided by the College Board®. These general chronological divisions should permit you the greatest chance of practicing your skills within the context of the particular period of history being studied in your class.

So let's get started. Part 1 begins by demystifying the AP essay rubrics and outlining the writing process. In Part 2, we break down each step and provide dozens of practice exercises so you can master the process. Finally, we introduce the new Multiple-Choice Question format and tackle the new Short-Answer Question type. Read and practice the steps, read your textbook, take good notes in class, and by May, you will be prepared to achieve the highest score on the AP European History exam. Good luck and write on!

Tony Maccarella

How to Use this Book

Guided Practice

Mastering the Essay contains Guided Practice exercises to help you understand the six steps of the *MTE* writing process found in Part 2 of this book. Each Guided Practice activity connects to a set of exercises in the Exercise Workbook (see the back cover for more information about the Exercise Workbook).

Chronological Periods

Because most European History teachers deliver their courses chronologically, each set of exercises contains skills-based items organized into chronological eras. This organization will help you to apply the information you are learning in school to each of the writing-skills exercises.

Choices

New skills will be introduced in each chapter, while skills learned in earlier chapters are continually reinforced. You may choose to practice each step of the writing process using the exercises most appropriate to the historical content your class is covering at that moment. Or you may choose to complete all the exercises in the workbook and develop good writing habits, while reviewing *all* aspects of European history. The choice is yours.

Additional Resources

Visit the companion website for additional resources and valuable updates!

www.sherpalearning.com/mte

Part 1
Before You Begin

The Key to the AP Exam

A few years ago, in my first AP* textbook, I argued that "the only skill that truly matters on the AP European History exam is writing." Now, however, the AP European History exam has changed, so it's time to reevaluate. The redesigned exam has fewer Multiple Choice Questions, a new Document-Based Question format, a single Free-Response Question (now called the Long Essay Question), and several Short-Answer Questions. So guess what? On the new exam, writing matters even more!

Most other books claiming to help improve your AP exam score are based on the assumption that success on the exam depends on your ability to recall historical facts. That is why so many of them devote hundreds of pages to reviewing historical content. Unfortunately, this assumption ignores several interesting statistics published by the College Board®, the organization that writes, administers, and scores the AP exam.

Did you know, for instance, that more than half of all students who scored a 4 or 5 on the old AP exam actually scored lower than 60% on the multiple-choice section[1] (the part of the test in which content seems to matter most)? This means that the majority of students whose scores qualify them for college credit get almost half of the Multiple-Choice Questions wrong. They did, however, achieve a top score on their essays. At the same time, many students who scored better than 50% on the multiple-choice section ended up getting a score of less than 4 on the exam, overall, if their essay scores were low.[2] **Bottom line—the key to a great score on the AP exam is good writing!**

I help score the essays for the AP European History exam. I know, from years of firsthand experience, what it takes to earn a top score on AP history essays, and I've written this book to share that

---

1, 2 – http://research.collegeboard.org/programs/ap/data

knowledge with students and teachers. The process outlined in this book is not a secret formula and the College Board® will not disqualify your score for using this process. In fact, the creators of the test want you to know how to write better essays. Better essays mean higher scores, and higher scores demonstrate to colleges and universities the value of an Advanced Placement education. Just as it is not a secret formula, this process is also not a magic potion. Just reading this book will not improve your score. Before you can see any real improvement in your score, you must practice—and master—the steps of the MTE writing process. That is precisely the reason why this book includes 100+ exercises, including 30 full-length Document-Based Questions (DBQs).

Let's be clear about one thing before we move ahead: just because writing is the key to a great score, that doesn't let you off the hook when it comes to studying. **Read your textbook!** You must know your history in order to achieve the highest scores on your essays. Content is not the key to the exam, but it still matters.

Understanding the Process

Considering that I've written a book about how to write strong, high-scoring essays, you might think that my students spend hours each week writing essay after essay. Not so. In fact, many of my students become uneasy when, for the first several months of the school year, they've been asked to write few, if any, full-length essays. During those months, they practice developing strong thesis statements and outlines—but no essays. By winter recess, some of them are actually a bit anxious, fearing that they should have been writing more.

It's not until the second semester rolls around that I ask them to try their hands at a complete essay. When they do, they are pleasantly surprised with the results. This is because, by that time, they have learned the most important lesson for mastering the essay: in order to produce a quality essay, it is essential to perfect the thesis and outline first.

To understand my reasoning, take a look at the AP Long Essay Question rubric. Of the 6 possible points awarded for the LEQ:

1 point is available in Part A – Thesis

1 point can be earned in Part B – Contextualization (essentially, framing your argument)

2 points are possible in Part D – Analysis & Reasoning (the logic & complexity of your argument)

That's 4 out of 6 points for thesis and argument—all the result of careful prewriting, which is evident in the opening paragraph of your essay. The remaining 2 points are awarded for Evidence Analysis, and although that is certainly best accomplished within the body of the essay, effective evidence analysis results from combining evidence you've brainstormed from the outset with the argument you've developed in your opening.

Even though the new essay rubrics look very different from those used with the old exam, in fact, these new rubrics award points for exactly the same key characteristics that make any essay great— *thesis, organization,* and *evidence.* And just as in the past, two of those three can be established in the opening paragraph, before any specific evidence is introduced.

Readers of AP exam essays consistently point to the thesis as the key feature in determining the quality of an essay. A high-quality thesis does more than simply answer the question; it outlines the argument in terms of how you will present evidence and why that evidence matters. After reading a high-quality thesis, the AP reader will have a fairly reliable idea of where the essay will fall on the rubric, in terms of thesis and organization. This is why my students spend half the year writing only theses and outlines. By February, they are skilled at developing two of the three key characteristics assessed on the LEQ rubric. Since they have completed most of the course content by that time, they have all the necessary evidence to tackle the third characteristic with very little trouble.

Is it possible to begin with a weak thesis and improve the essay within the body paragraphs? Yes, but without a well-organized opening, it is much more difficult to develop your argument. Remember that AP readers are humans, and all humans are subject to their own predispositions. Appeal to those predispositions! Take the time to craft a solid thesis and use it to develop a well-organized and comprehensive essay that your readers will appreciate. Since many of the AP readers are university professors, it should be no surprise that success on your college essays will rely very heavily on the same key characteristics found in your AP essays.

Introduction to the AP Rubrics

Like many other writing rubrics, the AP rubrics are designed to standardize the scoring process. In other words, they make the essays "more fair." Their design allows hundreds of trained readers to assess each essay in exactly the same way. That means, no matter who reads your essay, you are likely to achieve the same score. As you might imagine, any rubric that yields this level of consistency is also quite predictable. If you are trained to use the AP rubrics, you can identify the characteristics of a strong essay; and if you can identify the things that make a strong essay, you will find it easier to include those things within your own work.

As mentioned above, the AP rubrics have been redesigned. The new rubrics look very different from those we have used for the past decade or so. As you might expect, teachers who have worked with AP for a while have spent the past three years critiquing these new rubrics. In fact, the College Board® has responded with several tweaks to improve the new rubrics. But don't worry! Good writing is still good writing, and a well-written thesis essay will still be rewarded on the AP European History exam. While many have argued that all sorts of politics and bureaucratic haggling went into the new rubric structure established by the College Board®, above all the din sits one supreme truth—the AP exam must remain relevant to the demands of higher education if it is to survive. If you remember this one truth, you will have no trouble understanding why any AP essay rubric will ultimately reward the attributes most closely associated with excellent college essays. So, relax about the changes and let's dive in and learn more about the rubrics.

As discussed earlier, there are two essay questions on the AP European History exam—the Long Essay Question (LEQ) and the Document-Based Question (DBQ). Unlike the old essays, responses to the new questions are scored neither holistically, nor on a core checklist. The new rubrics utilize a hybrid format, but the easiest way to understand them might be to forget about their format and just look closely at the descriptive text within each rubric category.

AP European History LEQ Rubric

The LEQ rubric is divided into the following four parts: **Thesis, Contextualization, Evidence,** and **Analysis & Reasoning**. Let's start with the most essential piece of any thesis essay—the thesis.

Thesis (1 point)

In order to earn the one point assigned in the Thesis section of the rubric, you must create a thesis statement that responds directly to all parts of the question, and you must place that statement within your opening or closing paragraph. That's it! Simply answer the question and write your answer in the first or last paragraph. But, don't forget that an excellent thesis might help you to earn an additional point or two in the fourth part of the rubric—Analysis & Reasoning.

Contextualization (1 point)

In addition to developing a logical argument that demonstrates a complete understanding of the specific question you've chosen to answer, the College Board® wants you to demonstrate an understanding of the historical context of your argument. If you open your essay with a few statements that describe the historical setting within which your argument is best understood, you will earn this point. We will address several of the best options for accomplishing this goal.

Evidence (2 points)

The Evidence section of the rubric is the part that rewards you for all those long hours spent memorizing details. If you mention a few specific examples with relevance to the question prompt, you can earn the first of the two points. If you connect that evidence to your thesis, you will get the second point, as well. *Mastering the*

Essay devotes an entire unit to evidence and its use within your argument, so these points will be yours, too.

Analysis & Reasoning (2 points)

The College Board® wants students to demonstrate an ability to think like professional historians. To that end, the rubrics seek to reward specific historical argument techniques—*Comparison*, *Causation*, and *Change and Continuity Over Time* (CCOT). Depending on the essay prompt, you must create a response that takes the form of one of these specific argument-types.

Since your thesis tells the reader what you intend to say, and an analytical thesis describes how you will make your argument, your thesis can help you earn the two points in the Analysis & Reasoning section of the rubric (that's in addition to the one point earned in the Thesis section). To illustrate, let's look at Causation. You can earn one point for developing and supporting an argument that describes a cause/effect of a historical development/process. The second point is awarded to an argument that explains the reasons for that cause/effect. Any acceptable thesis will develop the argument, and an analytical thesis will list the reasons. So, an *excellent* analytical thesis will include almost everything you need for three of the six total points on the LEQ rubric.

AP European History DBQ Rubric

Like the LEQ rubric, the DBQ rubric is divided into the same four parts—**Thesis**, **Contextualization**, **Evidence**, and **Analysis & Reasoning**.

Thesis (1 point)

The DBQ thesis is constructed in the same way as that of the LEQ. You earn one point for addressing all parts of the question directly.

Contextualization (1 point)

Just as with the LEQ, the College Board® wants you to demonstrate an understanding of the historical context of your DBQ argument. Include a few statements describing the historical setting for your argument in the opening paragraph, and you will earn this point. More on this in Step 5.

Evidence (3 points)

Since the DBQ is document-based, you are rewarded for your use of the documents. You will earn one point for using the content of at least three documents to address the topic of the question. If you use at least six documents in support of your thesis, you will get a second point.

The third point is awarded for using at least one specific outside example—not a part of or from the documents—to support or qualify your argument. We will spend a good deal of time discussing evidence when we get to the body of the DBQ in Step 5.

Analysis & Reasoning (2 points)

The first of these points is awarded for a critical analysis of the sources in at least three of the documents (this used to be called Point-of-View, or POV). We will address this topic in detail as you progress through the steps of the writing process.

Just like on the LEQ, you can earn the second point of Analysis & Reasoning by demonstrating an ability to think like a professional historian by developing a complex argument utilizing the one of these historical argument techniques— *Comparison, Causation,* and *Change and Continuity Over Time* (CCOT).

Although the new rubrics are divided into distinct sections, the characteristics of any particular essay may cross over the borders of these sections. So, in theory, an essay with a clear, analytical thesis and a generally persuasive argument, but only one piece of specific evidence in support of each category, may receive the same score as an essay that contains a clear thesis that is less than analytical, but includes a very persuasive analysis of considerable evidence.

In practice, however, the essay with the stronger thesis has an advantage. The thesis is the reader's primary guide to understanding the author's argument. Consequently, on the AP exam, as in many college classes, **the thesis is viewed as a reliable predictor of the overall strength of the argument**. A weak thesis usually indicates a weak argument, whereas a clear, analytical thesis often indicates a strong argument. The reader (whether an AP scorer or college professor) is predisposed to awarding the higher score to the essay with the better thesis. It is for this reason that you should spend a good deal of time honing your thesis-writing skills.

Sample Essays for Evaluation

Now that you are familiar with the LEQ rubric and the DBQ rubric, it is time to look at some sample essays. See if you can determine why some essays are more successful than others. Read the Long Essay Question example and the three sample responses that follow it. Use the LEQ rubric guide in the previous section to help you score each essay. Be sure to evaluate the sample essay for each point-category in the rubric—Thesis, Contextualization, Evidence, and Analysis & Reasoning.

> **Example Question:** In what ways does Leonardo da Vinci deserve the title, Renaissance Man?

Essay #1

For centuries, medieval Europe took its cues from the Roman Catholic Church. Medieval scholars and artists adhered to a set of values that dictated a strict social order, a focus on the afterlife, and anonymity in the eyes of God. At the start of the 14th century, Italian artists, influenced by exposure to previously unknown ancient Greek and Roman works, began to push against the values of medieval society. The Italian Renaissance was founded on the values of generalism, humanism, and individualism, and Leonardo da Vinci, as an exemplar of these new values, deserves the title, *Renaissance Man*. As a painter, writer, inventor, and scientist, he was the consummate generalist. His use of new artistic techniques to glorify the human form makes him an exemplary humanist. Like so many of the artists of the Italian Renaissance, Leonardo's individualism was obvious in his constant battle to distinguish himself, and his work, as different from and better than that of his peers.

Many Italian Renaissance painters dabbled in other fields, like writing and engineering, but Leonardo mastered more arts and sciences than anyone else of his time. *The Last Supper* and *Mona Lisa* are the best examples of his artistic talents, and these works are still listed with those of Raphael and Michelangelo as among the greatest paintings of the Renaissance. Among his best known writings is *On Painting*, in which he glorifies the painter and demeans the sculptor (the one art he never mastered). In addition to art, Leonardo is well-known for his military engineering, evidenced in his notebooks, and his scientific studies of the human body, which led to the famous sketch, *Vitruvian Man*.

Leonardo's anatomical sketches demonstrate his interest in not just medical sciences, but also the accurate portrayal of the human form in his art. Like Michelangelo, Leonardo dissected corpses to learn firsthand the structure of human muscles so he could better represent them under the skin of his subjects. He also mastered the techniques of perspective and chiaroscuro in order to more accurately depict humanity and human society. This attention to the details of human life contrasted with works of the previous century that focused on Christian symbolism with little regard for realism.

Another major difference between Italian Renaissance artists and those of the pre-Renaissance centuries was a desire for individual renown. Leonardo, like his peers, did all he could to insure that he received credit for his own work. In addition to signing many of his works, he is most famous for writing in reverse in his notebooks, so that his notes could only be read in a mirror. This was Leonardo's best attempt at copyright.

With the *Mona Lisa*, *On Painting*, and *Vitruvian Man*, Leonardo da Vinci exemplified generalism and set himself apart from his peers as perhaps the most well-rounded artist of the Italian Renaissance. He used scientific study and cutting edge artistic techniques to better illuminate the human form, making him a favorite among humanists. Finally, the simple fact that he wrote in mirror-image in his notebooks to insure that he would always be credited for his own ideas is strong evidence that he valued individualism. Generalism, humanism, and individualism— all values of the Italian Renaissance—were combined to perfection within the best example of a Renaissance Man, Leonardo da Vinci.

Essay #2

Leonardo da Vinci was definitely a Renaissance Man. Other artists were great painters, sculptors, architects, or inventors, but Leonardo was all of these things. That makes him the best example of a Renaissance Man—someone who does everything.

Leonardo painted the *Mona Lisa* and many other great paintings. His paintings are considered some of the best of the Renaissance, but he was not satisfied with being one of the best painters ever. He also learned how to sculpt and write. Besides art, Leonardo designed churches and other buildings, making him a great architect. And he is very well-known for his inventions, like the bicycle, the machine gun, and the helicopter.

Leonardo da Vinci was definitely a Renaissance Man.

Essay #3

There were many great artists during the Italian Renaissance, but one of the best was Leonardo da Vinci. He was a great artist, a writer, a scientist, and one of the best inventors of his time.

As an artist, Leonardo was considered one of the best in Italy at that time. He painted the *Mona Lisa*, which may have been a self-portrait, and *The Last Supper*. In both of these great paintings, he used perspective and chiaroscuro, cutting-edge techniques, to make his work more realistic. Leonardo was so great that one time he and Michelangelo competed for the chance to fresco a building in Florence, and Leonardo won with his sketch of the Battle of Cascina. In addition to being a great painter, he also wrote a book about painting called *On Painting*.

Leonardo was also a great scientist. Among his many experiments were several dissections. He and Michelangelo both dissected human cadavers in order to study the muscles of the human body so they could do a better job of painting humans. He learned so much about human anatomy that he was able to draw *Vitruvian Man*, a perfectly proportioned human model.

One of the greatest things about Leonardo da Vinci was his inventions. He invented a bicycle, a helicopter, and several machine guns. Although he never actually built any of these things, his ideas were preserved in his notebooks, and we know they were his because he wrote all his notes backwards so nobody else could steal them. Also, people today have built many of his inventions as part of a TV show and they almost all work!

There is no doubt that Leonardo da Vinci was one of the greatest, if not THE greatest, artists of the Italian Renaissance. He was a painter, writer, scientist, and inventor. Most other Renaissance artists barely mastered one of those things, but Leonardo was great at all of them.

Sample Essay Scores and Rationale

Now that you have evaluated and scored each of the three sample essays, review the scores and study the explanations as to why each essay received the score that it did. Then review your own answers and see how close you came to awarding the correct score.

Comments on Essay #1

This essay is probably a 6. The author has clearly addressed the tasks and terms in the opening paragraph. After a brief summary of the medieval world view to contextualize the argument, the thesis not only states WHAT the author wants to say, but also HOW the argument will be structured. Additionally, the rest of the opening paragraph goes into WHY this argument seems to make sense, so the thesis is clear and analytical, describing the relative significance of Leonardo da Vinci—3 points so far. The body paragraphs follow the diagram laid out in the opening, with one paragraph for each of the three categories of evidence— generalism, humanism, and individualism. The author includes many specific examples within each category, and in each case, analyzes the evidence by stating WHY it matters to the thesis—2 more points. Finally, the author analyzes evidence to corroborate and qualify the argument, demonstrating an understanding of the complexities of history. The thesis is clear and analytical, the organization is clear and logical, the argument is complex, persuasive and well-supported. This is a top-ranking essay.

Comments on Essay #2

This is the shortest of the three and it earns a 3. It has a thesis that addresses the tasks and terms of the question, though only superficially. The author makes the thesis slightly better than a simple restatement of the question by including a definition of *Renaissance Man* – 1 point. The rest of the opening contrasts da Vinci with other artists of the Renaissance, which helps to explain his relative significance – 1 point. In terms of evidence, the essay falls far short of adequate, but does include a few specifics—*Mona Lisa*, machine gun, etc.—with little analysis – 1 point. Although some of the evidence is erroneous—da Vinci was not a renowned sculptor— the errors will not detract enough to impact the essay's already middling score. Finally, there is no attempt at historical context. Minimal thesis, few specifics, little analysis, and no contextualization—this essay earns a 3.

Comments on Essay #3

It is clear that the author of this essay knows something significant about the Italian Renaissance. Unfortunately, one thing the author does not know is how to answer an LEQ on the AP exam. The essay is very clearly organized and includes several pieces of specific evidence, but all the analysis is directed at demonstrating da Vinci's greatness. The author states very clearly in the opening that da Vinci is one of the greatest artists of the Renaissance, and develops a fairly persuasive argument to demonstrate this point. The problem is that the term to be assessed in this question is "Renaissance Man," not "great artist." AP readers are specifically trained to avoid doing the analysis for the student. Analysis must be explicit within the essay in order to earn credit. This author may have understood the topic, but ignored the tasks and terms in the essay, thus misinterpreting the question—so the essay fails to earn the Thesis point. Because the rubric allows for the use of evidence "relevant to the topic of the prompt," this essay could earn one Evidence point but nothing else. This essay earns a 1.

Taking the Next Step

Having reviewed and considered the sample essays, it is now time to examine and practice the process used to compose successful LEQ and DBQ essays. Begin by studying the writing process outlines that follow in the beginning of Part 2.

Part 2
The MTE Process

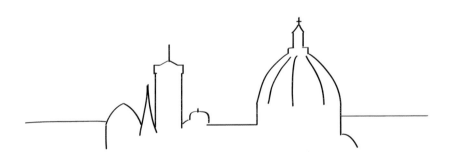

The Writing Process
—An Overview

The LEQ Writing Process

Step 1: Analyze the Question

Read the prompt and identify the tasks and terms.

Step 2: Organize the Evidence

A. Brainstorm for essential evidence.
B. Organize the evidence into categories, addressing all tasks and terms.
C. Use the categories to create an outline of your argument.

Step 3: Develop the Thesis

Create a thesis that addresses all tasks and terms of the question and uses three categories of evidence to clearly state your argument.

Step 4: Write the Opening

Draft an opening paragraph that includes the thesis and connects each category to the thesis with brief analysis (*why?* or *how?*).
The opening paragraph should outline your argument and frame it within some historical context..

Step 5: Write the Body

Topic sentences from each paragraph should expand on the category statements in the opening. All evidence must relate back to the thesis (*why does this matter to the argument?*)

Step 6: Write the Closing

Close the essay by restating the opening and alluding to the best evidence from the body.

The DBQ Writing Process

Step 1: Analyze the Question

Read the prompt and identify the tasks and terms.

Step 2: Analyze the Documents

A. Read the documents, taking notes in the margin.

B. Apply the 3-Step Document Analysis process to each document:

❶ **Summarize:** What does the document say?

❷ **Analyze:** Why does the document matter to the tasks and terms?

❸ **Criticize:** How might the source affect the meaning of the document?

C. Brainstorm outside evidence to supplement the documents.

D. Group the documents and outside evidence into 3+ logical categories.

Step 3: Develop the Thesis

Create a thesis that addresses all tasks and terms of the question and uses three categories of evidence to clearly state your argument.

Step 4: Write the Opening

Draft an opening paragraph that includes the thesis and connects each category to the thesis with brief analysis (*why?* or *how?*). The opening paragraph should outline your argument and frame it within some historical context.

Step 5: Write the Body

Topic sentences from each paragraph should expand on the category statements in the opening. Analyze each (and every) document individually, as well as any specific evidence outside the document set, connecting each document and piece of evidence back to the thesis. Include source analysis (whenever possible) and document citations.

Step 6: Write the Closing

Close the essay by restating the opening and alluding to the best evidence from the body.

Analyzing the Question

When I was younger, I lived with my grandparents for a few years. I was in my first years teaching—young, single, and broke. Nanny and Pop-Pop (that's what I'd always called them, for as long as I can remember) were in their eighties—grey-haired, slower, and quite a bit shorter than they had been in their youth. I needed a cheap place to sleep and they needed a little help taking care of their three-story home. It was the perfect arrangement! I enjoyed regular home-cooked meals and clean laundry, and they had someone to do repairs, lift heavy things, and reach the little glasses on the top shelf of the cupboard.

I have many fond memories of my time with Nanny and Pop-Pop, and not-just-a-few of those memories form the basis for some of my best party bits. One incident that makes me laugh whenever I think of it involves sitting at the kitchen table with Pop while Nanny was preparing some delicious meal at the sink. This scene repeated itself three times a day, every day. Neither of my grandparents had particularly good hearing by the time I had moved in with them, so their conversations were often a bit like Abbot and Costello's "Who's on First" routine. Nanny would stand at the sink with her back to the kitchen while Pop and I were seated at the little kitchen table at the other end of the room—completely out of her sight. He might say to me, "Tony, if you have some time today, I need to go shopping." (I became Pop's chauffer after he'd given up his driver's license.) Nanny, unable to see—or hear—either one of us, but certain that Pop was saying something disparaging about her, would interject, "Now, Angelo! Tell the truth! I asked you to move those boxes last week. You said you were busy, so I moved them myself." Pop would roll his eyes at me, having heard only some of her complaint, and say, "Ruth! You can't hear a damn thing I say, can you? I don't care if you already did some shopping, the Acme has a sale on Tide and I don't want to miss it!" Nanny's retort was quick and equally disjointed, "Sure you can go for a ride, but do you have to go now? Tony's busy! Why don't you wait until later?" By this time, Pop was already standing at the door wearing his light canvas jacket and plaid newsboy cap, and running out of patience for what he considered to be Nanny's irrational nagging. "I can't wait! The sale is only today! Why can't you just mind your own business over there and give me a minute of peace!"

Although their banter was always entertaining and the memory of it still makes me chuckle, in terms of communication, it was quite ineffective. Neither one of my grandparents really understood what the other was saying (because they couldn't hear each other).

Unfortunately, my grandparents' arguments are a little like the AP exam—only not as tall. The quality of your AP essays depends largely on your clear understanding of the question. The College Board® cites misreading the question as one of the most common mistakes among AP students. Before you can develop an excellent answer, you have to be certain that you understand exactly what you've been asked to do—you must learn to analyze the tasks and terms.

TASKS: What to Do

We define TASKS as those parts of the question that tell you WHAT TO DO. The task will ask you to apply what you know about a particular period of history in a specific way. Take a look at the essay prompt below.

> ***Example Question:*** *Identify and analyze the characteristics of 15th-century Italian city-states that made them fertile grounds for Renaissance artists.*

What is this prompt telling you to do? For this question, the tasks are "identify" and "analyze." Most AP European History essay questions identify the task with a specific verb:

Assess the extent to which Napoleon I was anti-revolutionary.

Discuss the arguments in favor of a common currency in Europe, 1980–2000.

Analyze the impact of the Industrial Revolution on the lower classes of Europe in the nineteenth century.

Some questions may require that you complete more than one task, but in every case, the question will pose your tasks explicitly.

Compare and *contrast* the influence of nationalism on Italian and German unification.

Describe and *analyze* the components of the Catholic Reformation in Spain.

Study the verbs in the sample questions above and make certain that you understand their meanings. Then, see if you can define or paraphrase each question.

assess—to understand the impact or importance of

discuss—to elaborate or explain

analyze—to explain the meaning or importance of something for something else

compare and *contrast*—to relate in terms of how one thing is like or not like another

describe—to elaborate or clarify in terms of greater detail

Make certain that you clearly understand what each one of these tasks requires you to do. Later in this book, you will learn how to respond to questions that use a slightly different format.

TERMS: What to Discuss

The TERMS of the question determine the scope of your answer. In other words, the terms are defined as those parts of the question that specify WHAT TO DISCUSS. Each question introduces a body of material that collectively forms the general subject of the essay. The terms are the words used to focus the subject of the question. These terms should elicit a body of knowledge from you that will serve as evidence later on. As you probe the terms, you should be able to start to formulate categories of evidence that will help you to develop your thesis and outline your argument.

Take a look at the example question prompt again.

> **Example Question:** Identify and analyze the characteristics of 15th-century Italian city-states that made them fertile grounds for Renaissance artists.

What are the specific topics you are asked to address in this prompt? In this question, the terms are "characteristics of Italian city-states," "fertile grounds," and "Renaissance artists."

Taking the Next Step

Once you've analyzed the question and you understand the tasks and terms, then it's time to call upon your knowledge of history to brainstorm and organize the evidence you will need to thoroughly address the terms of the question. The way you organize your evidence will determine your categories of evidence and the foundation of your thesis. The thesis is the most important sentence in your entire essay, so anything that contributes to the quality of that sentence is something with which you must be concerned. But don't be afraid, just turn the page and let's get to work.

Organizing the Evidence

In 1296, foundations were laid for a massive cathedral in Florence, Italy. Santa Maria del Fiore was intended to be the greatest architectural structure in all of Christendom, surpassing the great gothic cathedrals of France, Germany, and Milan. According to its original designer, Arnolfo di Cambio, the entire edifice would be crowned with a dome, the size of which would outshine even that of Santa Sophia in Europe's grandest city, Constantinople. The Commune of Florence accepted Cambio's plans, leveled forests for the necessary timber, and began floating marble down the Arno for the façade. Although Florentines agreed that the new cathedral should be, "a more beautiful and honorable temple than any in any other part of Tuscany," they understood one important problem from the outset—no one anywhere in their world of the 14th century knew how to erect a dome sufficiently large enough to cover the apse of this new cathedral. The solution would not be found until 1418—over one hundred years later—and even then, it remained untested until completion of the dome in the 1430s.

Why would a city with the resources of Florence in the 13th and 14th centuries accept a design for a structure that no one knew how to build? The answer lies in their faith—faith in the help of God and faith in the pace of innovation. They believed that God would assist them in finding someone, someday, with the knowledge and skills necessary to complete the dome, and 140 years later, their faith paid off. But wasn't that really risky? What if it had been discovered that the span of the dome was physically too large to vault and the task impossible? For starters, 140 years of building would have ended in embarrassment.

Fortunately, things turned out okay for Florence, but it took more than a century to figure out. Even still, the result could have gone the other way since no one was certain it was even possible. *Why am I telling you this?* There's a lesson to be learned here that you need to remember when writing your AP essays—don't plan an essay for which you lack the necessary skills and resources. You don't have 140 years to wait for the answer!

By mid-year in my AP Euro class, it is not unusual for some students to write beautiful thesis statements, only to fall flat on their faces in the body of the essay because their arguments lack sufficient relevant evidence. These same students will complain that they weren't able to defend their theses because they "didn't learn enough" in order to do so. The problem these students have is not a lack of sufficient evidence to support a good thesis, but rather a thesis that fails to account for the available evidence.

As smart students learn the skills of great writing, they find it easier and easier to develop good arguments in response to any essay question. So easy, in fact, that often these very knowledgeable writers skip prewriting altogether and jump right into the essay. This is a big problem! Because brainstorming evidence is part of prewriting, skipping this part of the process means that you will begin your essay before you have gathered the necessary evidence to address the terms of the question. For example, I may know—in general terms—that Michelangelo was moody, antisocial, and a perfectionist, and that it was these qualities that led him to complete the ceiling of the Sistine Chapel without the assistance of a complete studio of artists. But, without specific evidence connecting these character traits to the artist's decisions regarding the Sistine Chapel, any essay using those reasons (categories of evidence) will be relegated to broad generalizations with little support—not the best situation for an AP essay. I would do much better to begin by listing the specific evidence I actually know and then developing my categories of evidence from that list. My essay might not be the argument I wanted to make, but it will be well organized and well supported.

In this section, we will look at sample AP Long Essay Questions (LEQs). For each example, you will be asked to generate a list of specifics that you believe may be relevant to the terms of the question. You will then learn to organize your evidence into relevant categories and develop a persuasive thesis from those categories.

Right now you're probably panicking because you may feel unprepared to list specifics for all these examples. No worries! The sample questions are arranged into chronological topics that likely parallel those covered within your class, so start with whatever content you feel most comfortable. Additionally, every question is accompanied by an illustration of my own process. Although your ideas may be different, I hope my models will prove helpful. If, after all of this, you are simply blanking on some topics, *Mastering the Essay* includes a thorough list of key terms in the Appendix. Just look at the relevant time-period; the key terms should help kick-start your memory.

Brainstorming and Organizing Evidence

Too many students fail to provide enough specific, relevant evidence to adequately support their arguments. Often, their problem is not that they don't know their history, but rather that they can't think of the specific historical information necessary for their particular argument. The solution is simple—choose an argument for which you know the most specific evidence. To accomplish this seemingly herculean task, you need to start with the evidence and develop the argument around it.

Identify the Tasks and Terms

As you learned in the preceding section, the first step of the process is to analyze the question by identifying the tasks and terms. Remember, we define *tasks* as those parts of the question that tell you what to do. *Terms* are defined as those parts of the question that specify the topics to be discussed in your answer.

Brainstorm Essential Evidence

Once you understand the tasks and terms, you should begin listing specific bits of history that you think might apply to the question. Brainstorm as many relevant details as you can recall that clarify or elaborate on the terms of the question. These details will serve as evidence for your essay. As you write down these pieces of evidence, you will find that the information you have written down will jog your memory further, and you will have even more evidence to use in your essay.

Organize Evidence into Categories

Once the evidence is in front of you, begin to group these bits into categories that could be applied to the tasks and terms of your question. Start by framing questions around the terms: *How are these terms connected to each other? How might this evidence help to illustrate those connections?* The questions you pose will suggest categories—themes, concepts, and characteristics—that help to demonstrate your understanding of the terms.

Develop the Thesis

Finally, using these categories, develop a working thesis and begin to formulate your opening paragraph. This may sound oversimplified, but not to worry. We will spend plenty of time delving deeper into thesis statements in the next section of this book. For now, we will focus only on organizing the evidence into effective categories.

The following example should help you better understand the process of choosing and organizing the evidence you generate through brainstorming. As I hope you will see, it is not necessary to know every detail in order to score well on the essays. You need only know how to make the best argument possible with the details that you know and understand.

Guided Practice: Brainstorming and Organizing Evidence

Directions: Read the question and identify the tasks and terms. Then, brainstorm and organize the evidence you can remember into categories that help illustrate the connections among the tasks and terms.

> **Example Question:** *Identify and analyze the characteristics of 15th-century Italian city-states that made them fertile grounds for Renaissance artists.*

Tasks: Identify and analyze

Terms: 15th-century Italian city-states, fertile grounds, Renaissance artists

Although your memory of the Italian Renaissance may include details that are different from mine, the evidence below should help to illustrate the process. As I consider the terms individually, these are the details that come to mind:

Brainstorm Evidence:

Italian city-states:
Rome, Florence, Milan, Venice, Siena, Perugia

15th-century Italy:
Bourgeois, Medici, Sforza, humanists, popes, Roman ruins

Renaissance artists:
Michelangelo, Leonardo da Vinci, Titian, Brunelleschi, David, Last Supper, duomo

Next, I think about the connections among the tasks and terms of the question. What were some characteristics of Italian city-states? What made Italy ripe for artistic innovation? Again, my thoughts below may differ from yours, but should serve to illustrate the process:

- City-states were relatively autonomous in terms of government and finances
- City-states were controlled, at least in part, by bourgeoisie of great wealth
- City-states competed with each other for power and prestige
- 15th century humanism helped to rejuvenate an interest in ancient Greece and Rome
- Italy was home to the antiquities of ancient Greece and Rome
- Works of antiquity served as models for Renaissance artists

These ideas were generated from the specific details brainstormed above. Now let's try to form some logical order to help address the tasks and terms of the question:

Categories of Evidence:

- **Close proximity to antiquities** provided Italian artists with easy access to ancient models and ready materials [Ruins of the Roman Empire included marble columns and ancient sculptures]

- **Wealth of the bourgeois class** provided the money necessary to commission works from the greatest talents in Italy [Medici – Brunelleschi, Michelangelo, and Leonardo in Florence; Sforza – Leonardo in Milan; Della Rovere and Medici via the Papacy – Michelangelo in Rome]

- **Rivalries among city-states fueled by autonomy and pride** inspired a desire for more art and architecture to increase their collective grandeur [Milan – Leonardo da Vinci's The Last Supper; Florence – Brunelleschi's Dome and Michelangelo's David; Venice – Titian's works]

As we discussed earlier, these categories of evidence will form the structure of your essay. Later you will use them to construct your thesis. Remember, the thesis will tell the reader HOW you are going to answer the question. For now, here's a glimpse of one possible thesis for the example prompt using these categories.

> **Sample Thesis:** The coincidence of proximity to the works of antiquity, ready funding through local bourgeois wealth, and centuries-old intercity rivalries made the 15th-century Italian city-states a fertile ground for Renaissance artists.

We will discuss the characteristics that make this thesis effective in another section (Step 3).

Outlining an Argument

I have met many students who argue that outlining is too time-consuming, too cumbersome, and too useless to make any difference on their AP exam. These students invariably do not know how to outline an argument. Outlining should be a means to an end, not an end in itself. There is no need to use Roman numerals, parentheses, or indentations to form an outline for your argument. Think of the outline as a recipe, and the evidence as the ingredients. Organize the ingredients so that you will add them at the appropriate moments. Your outline might look like my grandmother's cookbook—circles and arrows and quick notes to yourself. Of course, it might also take a slightly more orderly form, like a chart (see "Analytical Thesis Development" in Step 3), but it will rarely look like an English assignment.

If you are still doubtful that "wasting" precious time outlining is a good idea, take another look at "Introduction to the AP Rubrics" in Part 1. You are unlikely to earn better than a 2 without a clear thesis and clear organization. Good planning enhances these characteristics, and one great way to plan your essay is by outlining. The ends justify the means.

Go back and review the Renaissance art example above. You can identify the evidence intended for the first, second, and third categories. Use this outline to clarify for yourself how and why this evidence might be useful. Draw whatever circles, arrows, and notes that you need to plan your essay, but make sure that your outline is neat enough to follow.

Taking the Next Step

Hold up! Before we move on to Step 3, "Writing the Thesis," we need to take a look at organizing evidence for a DBQ. The process is very similar to organizing evidence for the LEQ, but made somewhat easier by the test-makers because they've given you half of the evidence! We'll need to take a look at the details of document analysis and learn to effectively combine the evidence given by the DBQ with our own memory of history.

Analyzing the Documents

Although most students are a little afraid of the AP European History DBQ, my students come to absolutely love that section of the exam. Think about it—half of the evidence is provided for you, the tasks and terms are no more difficult than those in the Long Essay Questions, and the points in the rubric are essentially a checklist. What's not to like?

The real challenge to writing a great DBQ essay is understanding the documents used in the question. With some practice, this too will pose no real problem. Like the LEQ, you begin the DBQ by breaking down the question into its tasks and terms. Then, instead of brainstorming evidence, simply start reading the documents. As you read each one, think about the ways it might be used to address the tasks and terms of the question. Write notes next to each document to help you remember what you were thinking when you read it. You should also think about each document's origin, purpose, and author while you read it. Later on, we will talk more in-depth about these three elements when the process of document analysis is introduced.

As you go through this process, you will probably remember additional specific evidence that might be useful in your essay. List these other details as you did for the LEQ. When you identify specific groups of documents and other evidence that can be used to support your thesis, make notes about that, too. As you develop these categories of evidence, you should also begin to see a thesis developing. Write down your ideas about this thesis, as well. Eventually, you will have generated an informal outline like those from Step 2 (LEQ), and then you will be ready to begin writing your essay.

The test-makers give you 15 minutes to prewrite for your DBQ, but
don't worry if you haven't yet finished analyzing documents and
brainstorming evidence after this assigned reading period. You can
continue to prewrite even after the proctor distributes the essay
booklets. Remember, the rubric rewards clarity and organization, so
even if it takes 20–25 minutes to prepare your DBQ outline, you will
have enough time to finish writing—and your essay will be better for
the effort. Now let's look at the process, step by step, just like we did
for the LEQ.

Document Analysis—Getting Started

To better understand how to analyze the documents in a DBQ, let's
take look at an example DBQ prompt and practice document.

> **Example Question:** *Identify the leaders of the major European
> powers in 1914, and analyze the impact of these individuals on the
> start of the First World War.*

Document A

> **SOURCE: Wilhelm II, Kaiser of the German Empire, a letter to his
> cousin, Nicholas II, Czar of Russia, January 30, 1914.**
>
> Berlin 30/1/14
>
> Dearest Nicky
>
> Many thanks to you dear Alix and the children for your kind wishes and
> the lovely china pot which accompanied them. Thank God I could spend
> my birthday in happiness especially owing to the presence of dear Sophy
> and Georgy who had come all the way from Athen [Athens] to spend the
> day with me. I am most gratified that you still keep pleasant recollections
> of the visit you paid us last summer on the occasion of Sissy's wedding,
> and you may be assured that we all most heartily reciprocate your kind
> feelings and remembrance.
>
>   * * * *
>
> With best love to Alix and the dear children believe me, dearest Nicky
>
>   Ever your devoted cousin and friend
>
>   Willy

As always, we first identify the tasks and terms of the question.

Tasks: Identify AND Analyze

Terms: European Leaders in 1914, WWI, Impact of individuals

Now let's analyze the document together.

What does the document say about the LEADERS of the European powers?

The document focuses on the personal lives of Wilhelm and Nicholas and their families. Apparently, Nicholas sent Wilhelm a "china pot" for his birthday. It also indicates that Nicholas had visited Germany for a wedding in 1913. Wilhelm signs as "cousin and friend."

Why is the document important to our understanding of HOW or WHY the leaders impacted the start of the war?

The document really says nothing directly about state affairs or the impending crisis. If it is used in this essay, it will most likely support some point about the personal relationships among the leaders of Europe.

What do you know about the source of the document? How might the source have affected the meaning of the document?

Wilhelm II was the king of Germany in 1914. He was also cousin to Czar Nicholas of Russia. By January of 1914, France and Russia had been parties to a defensive alliance, the Entente Cordiale, for 20 years, and the British had joined in 1907 to form the Triple Entente. It is possible that Wilhelm, now surrounded by an alliance of potential enemies, was attempting to use his familial relationship with Nicholas to influence Russia's commitment to the Triple Entente.

That's it! I know, I know—you're sitting there thinking, "What's it?" How do you know what questions to ask? How do you know if your answers are correct? How do you finish all this pre-essay work in just a few minutes? How does all this help to write a DBQ essay on the AP Euro exam? Take a breath. Now read on and let's look at the fundamentals of document analysis.

The 3-Step Document Analysis Process

Document analysis can be a scary process, especially when it's presented as a seemingly random list of questions—like those in the previous section. If we look at the essence of document analysis, however, it really boils down to three very reasonable steps— **Summarize, Analyze, Criticize.** To better understand the logic behind this 3-Step Process, imagine that you are a spectator at a Final Four basketball game. The game is tight in the closing minutes and someone a few rows away yells something directly at you, but you didn't quite hear what they said. What do you do? First, and most importantly, you ask, "What did you say?" You can do nothing before you know what was said. Then, as you interpret the meaning of the words, you ask yourself, "Why does this matter to me?" Maybe the person yelled, "Do you want a hotdog?" It's the end of the game, so those words may not matter. But maybe the person yelled, "Your hair is on fire!" That might matter more. Finally, as you decode the significance of the words, you account for the speaker. Who is this person and why is he talking to me? Might there be some other meaning to these words in this context?

The **3-Step Process** is just like that basketball game. When you approach a document for the first time, you have to ask, "What does it say?" This is step 1 – **Summarize.** Once you understand the document, you have to decide, "Why does it matter?" This is step 2 – **Analyze.** Finally, you have to consider the source. "How might this source have influenced the meaning of this document?" This is step 3 – **Criticize.**

> Get additional practice using the 3-Step Process in
> — MASTERING DOCUMENT ANALYSIS —
> See page 123 for more information.

Now try to follow these steps as you go through the example exercise below.

Guided Practice: Using the 3-Step Process to Analyze Documents for the DBQ

Directions: Identify the tasks and terms in the following question, and then use the 3-Step Process to determine how each document might address those tasks and terms. Write your notes in the margins. As you analyze the documents, make a list of other specific evidence that comes to mind.

> **Exercise Question:** *To what extent did the long-standing disputes between Eastern and Western Christendom contribute to the fall of Constantinople in 1453?*

Document A

SOURCE: Pope Gregory VII in a letter written to Ebouly de Rossi, 1073

It is far better for a country to remain under the rule of Islam than be governed by Christians who refuse to acknowledge the rights of the Catholic Church.

Document B

SOURCE: St. Mark Eugenicus, 15th-century Greek Orthodox theologian

Flee from the papists as you would from a snake and from the flames of a fire.

Document C

SOURCE: **Pope Nicholas V to Constantine XI (Byzantine Emperor), 1452**

If you, with your nobles and the people of Constantinople accept the decree of union, you will find Us and Our venerable brothers, the cardinals of the Holy Roman Church, ever eager to support your honor and your empire. But if you and your people refuse to accept the decree, you will force Us to take such measures as are necessary for your salvation and Our honor.

Document D

SOURCE: **George of Hungary, prisoner of the Ottomans 1436-1458, written c. 1453**

When recruiting for the army is begun, they gather with such readiness and speed you might think they are invited to a wedding not a war... those left at home feel an injustice has been done to them. They claim they will be happier if they die on the battlefield among the spears and arrows of the enemy than at home.... .

Document E

SOURCE: **Chalcocondylas, Byzantine chronicler on the Ottoman soldiers, 1453**

There is no prince who has his armies and camps in better order, both in abundance of victuals and in the beautiful order they use in encamping without any confusion or embarrassment.

Document F

SOURCE: **Leonard of Chios, Genoese archbishop of Mytilene, letter to Pope Nicholas V, 1453**

I can testify that Greeks, Latins, Germans, Hungarians, Bohemians and men from all the Christian countries were on the side of the Turks ... Oh, the wickedness of denying Christ like this!

Document G

SOURCE: **George Sphrantzes, Fall of the Byzantine Empire: a chronicle, written c. 1470**

The emperor consented to have the pope's name commemorated in our services, by necessity, as we hoped to receive some aid. Whoever were willing would pronounce the commemoration in Saint Sophia; the rest would incur no blame and remain peaceful. These services took place on November 12. Six months later we had received as much aid from Rome as had been sent to us by the sultan of Cairo.

Explanation

So let's see how well you did.

For each document, you should have begun with **Summarize** by asking, "What does it say?" Then, **Analyze** by asking, "Why does it matter (to the tasks and terms of the question)?" (For example, What does each document say about the "long-standing disputes between Eastern and Western Christendom" or the "fall of Constantinople in 1453"? Does the document state or imply anything about HOW the disputes may have contributed to the fall?) Finally, **Criticize** by asking, "What do I know about this source and how might it have influenced the meaning of this document?"

Document A

SUMMARIZE – Pope Gregory would prefer that the Eastern Christians remain under Islamic control if they refuse to submit to Rome.

ANALYZE – As early as 1073, the East/West disputes seem to influence the pope's attitude about the Byzantine struggle against the Ottomans.

CRITICIZE – As leader of the Western Church at the time of the Great Schism, Pope Gregory may be trying to pressure Easterners to rejoin Rome.

Document B

SUMMARIZE – St. Mark compares the threat of the Roman Church to that of a snake or a fire.

ANALYZE – In the 1400s, the East/West disputes continue to be contentious.

CRITICIZE – As an Orthodox theologian, St. Mark's views may exemplify a wider view among Easterners.

Document C

SUMMARIZE – Pope Nicholas V poses reunification with Rome as a prerequisite for Western help in Constantinople.

ANALYZE – East/West disputes are apparently a significant barrier to cooperation, even in the face of Ottoman threats.

CRITICIZE – Nicholas, as pope, still holds the views of his predecessors of four centuries earlier.

Document D

SUMMARIZE – George of Hungary speaks well of the bravery of Ottoman soldiers.

ANALYZE – This document says nothing directly about the East/West disputes, but does lend credence to an alternative reason for the fall of Constantinople—Ottoman bravery.

CRITICIZE – A prisoner from the opposing army is unlikely to speak well of his enemy unless he was very impressed.

Document E

SUMMARIZE – Chalcondylas speaks well of the Ottoman army.

ANALYZE – This document supports an alternative reason for the fall of Constantinople, the strength of the Ottoman army.

CRITICIZE – Although his loyalty to the emperor is uncertain from the description "Byzantine chronicler," it is likely that Chalcocondylas would not overstate his praise of the enemy unless he was very impressed. In combination with Document D, this evidence is even stronger.

Document F

SUMMARIZE – Leonard of Chios says that Westerners helped the Ottoman army in the siege of Constantinople. He compares their assistance to denying Christ.

ANALYZE – Implies that the East/West disputes were more important than defending Christianity in 1453, and the disputes led to increased Ottoman military strength through direct assistance from the West.

CRITICIZE – A Roman Catholic bishop writing to the pope is unlikely to speak offensively. Because he described the Western help as "denying Christ," it may be that, at least officially, the pope would be unwilling to accept East/West disputes as justification for helping the infidel.

Document G

SUMMARIZE – Sphrantzes writes that the emperor agreed to commemorate the pope in religious services in Constantinople, presumably in exchange for help from the West, but no help ever came. He implies that the emperor acted honorably.

ANALYZE – Although the document makes no mention of the East/West disputes, it can be used to support the contention that the actions of the West contributed to the fall of Constantinople, no matter what the root cause of those actions may have been.

CRITICIZE – Sphrantzes, although not cited as such, can be assumed to be Byzantine based on his use of the first-person in the chronicle. This may help to explain his criticism of the West.

DBQ Categories of Evidence

Just as with the LEQ, your DBQ argument should be divided into three logical categories of evidence. The task is a bit easier with the DBQ because most of the evidence has been provided for you in the form of the documents. As you analyze the documents and brainstorm outside evidence, you should begin to see how some of it might be used to support a thesis.

In the example above, Documents A and B are both evidence of the intensity of the long-standing distrust and animosity between the churches of the East and the West. Documents C, F, and G attest to the fact that the Western Church may have used the Ottoman threat to gain some control over the Eastern Church. Documents D and E, on the other hand, lend credence to a counter argument that Mehmet's army was simply better than that of the Byzantines. Additional outside evidence might include specifics of the Great Schism, details of Venetian actions in the months leading up to the Fall of Constantinople, or further support for the strength and preparedness of the Ottoman army. So an outline of three logical categories might look like this:

The intensity of the East/West dispute

Docs A and B

Other specific evidence of the Great Schism

The West's use of the crisis to regain control of the East

Docs C, F, and G

Details of Venetian actions in the months leading up to the fall of Constantinople

The strength of the Ottoman army

Docs D and E

Other specific evidence of the strength and preparedness of the Ottoman army

Taking the Next Step

Now that you have analyzed the documents, brainstormed some outside evidence, and grouped everything into three logical categories of evidence, you should have no trouble developing a thesis and writing the opening paragraph. Since the thesis is such a critical piece of the essay, we will spend the next section of the book honing your thesis skills.

3

Constructing the Thesis

Ever wonder what a bunch of history teachers would talk about in their spare time? Probably not. But if you're even a little bit curious, when AP Readers are thrown together every year to score the exam essays, they spend a good bit of their time talking about thesis statements. Okay, so maybe not so much "talking about" as "lamenting the absence of."

Select teachers and professors of history are brought together every year by the wonderful people who produce the AP exams—the College Board®. Some of our families refer to the gathering as summer camp for history geeks. And although each year brings its own unique topics of conversation, one consistent theme is the thesis. Readers continually lament the apparent lack of thesis writing skills among AP European History students.

Many of us teach AP Euro ourselves, so we know our students are writing good thesis statements. What we wonder is why so many other students are unable to do the same. This question was one of the biggest reasons why I set out to write *Mastering the Essay*. I decided to share what I do in class within the pages of this book because I know that learning to write consistently good thesis statements is an utterly doable task for any student.

This unit will guide you through a process that my own students have followed for years with great results. First, we will identify the elements of a great thesis, and then you will learn to construct a variety of thesis types. At the end of the unit, you will be ready to respond to any AP European History question with a clear, analytical thesis worthy of a top score on the AP rubric.

The Art of the Thesis

As you read earlier in this text (several times), the thesis is the single most important part of the essay. AP European History Readers consistently say that the thesis is "the heart of the essay." If the thesis is strong, the essay is likely to be strong, as well. If the thesis is weak, the essay is probably weak, too.

If they're not still fresh in your mind, take a minute to review the first two steps of the process. Once again, start with the tasks of the question—what are you asked to do? Next, identify the terms of the question—what are you asked to discuss?

A good thesis attacks the tasks and terms head-on. Respond to the question directly by telling the reader why and/or how you will complete the tasks within the body of your essay by using the terms. Your thesis must address the terms of the question explicitly and directly, and outline, however briefly, the categories of evidence you will use to make your point. Although it is not absolutely necessary to use three categories of evidence in every essay, it is a good rule of thumb. This is why so many English teachers refer to thesis essays as 5-paragraph essays—one opening paragraph, three body paragraphs (one for each category of evidence), and one closing paragraph.

Next, let's review the categories of evidence we created for the example prompt in Step 2 (LEQ).

Example Question: *Identify and analyze the characteristics of 15th-century Italian city-states that made them fertile grounds for Renaissance artists.*

Tasks: Identify and analyze

Terms: 15th-century Italian city-states, fertile grounds, Renaissance artists

Categories of Evidence:

- Rivalries among city-states fueled by autonomy and pride
- Proximity to antiquities
- Wealth of the bourgeois class

As we discussed earlier, these categories of evidence will form the structure of your essay. Use them to construct your thesis. Remember, the thesis will tell the reader HOW you are going to answer the question. Take another look at one possible thesis for the example prompt.

Sample Thesis: The coincidence of proximity to the works of antiquity, ready funding through local bourgeois wealth, and centuries-old intercity rivalries made the 15th-century Italian city-states a fertile ground for Renaissance artists.

As you can see, this thesis effectively states how you are going to answer the question and outlines the argument you will make in the body of the essay.

Developing a successful thesis is integrally connected to how carefully you read and how clearly you understand the tasks and terms of the essay question. For that reason, the exercises for each of the following sections are grounded in sample essay questions. These sets of exercises are designed to help you master the art of creating a successful thesis. The first section provides a series of examples of theses and asks you to identify how each would score on an AP exam. The second set of exercises asks you to generate a successful thesis based upon the process that you just learned. As you complete each set of exercises, remember that you are building on a process that will help you to compose clear, analytical thesis statements and consistently successful essays.

In order to write an excellent thesis, it helps to know what one looks like. The exercise below contains a sample essay question followed by several possible thesis responses. Your job is to score each thesis statement according to the criteria outlined in the LEQ rubric. Before you begin, review the LEQ rubric guide on page 7 of Part 1 to familiarize yourself with the thesis qualities that correspond with each score.

Guided Practice: Thesis Recognition

Directions: Begin each exercise in this set by identifying the tasks and terms of the question (**Step 1**). Next, read the thesis statements below the question. Then, on the line beside each thesis, provide the score that you think it deserves. Since the rubric awards one point for an acceptable thesis and you can move toward an additional point for Analysis & Reasoning by outlining your argument with an analytical thesis, you should rate each thesis with a 0, 1, or 2.

Follow along with the sample exercise below to see how it's done. The sample exercise is followed by answers and explanations to illustrate the process.

Exercise Question: Analyze the ways in which Italian Renaissance art reflects Renaissance values. Cite specific works and artists in your response.

Tasks: Analyze, cite

Terms: Italian Renaissance art, reflects, Renaissance value, specific works and artists

Possible Thesis Statement Responses:

_____ **A.** Art of the Italian Renaissance reflected an interest in humanism and classicism.

_____ **B.** Italian artists, such as Michelangelo and Titian, reflected Renaissance values in their works through their use of humanist techniques, classical themes, and secular realism.

_____ **C.** Italian Renaissance art reflected Renaissance values in many ways.

_____ **D.** Italian Renaissance art reflected Renaissance values socially, politically, and economically.

_____ **E.** The Renaissance values of humanism, classicism, and individualism are reflected in the works of Italian Renaissance artists.

_____ **F.** The Renaissance values of humanism, classicism, and individualism are reflected in the works of Michelangelo and da Vinci.

_____ **G.** The works of Michelangelo, Da Vinci, and Titian reflected Renaissance values.

Explanation

A. (0 points) This is actually a tricky thesis because, although it goes beyond restating the question, it fails to make the necessary connections to ALL tasks and terms of the question. The author has implied that "humanism and classicism" are Renaissance values (which they are), but this connection is implicit only. Your thesis should address ALL tasks and terms of the question explicitly. Additionally, this thesis alludes to only two categories of evidence—humanism and classicism. Although there is no strict requirement for three categories of evidence, it is a widely accepted standard in thesis essay writing (e.g., the 5-paragraph essay).

B. (2 points) The author has addressed all tasks and terms of the question by identifying specific artists ("Michelangelo and Titian") as well as specific Renaissance values (humanism, classicism, and secularism). Furthermore, this thesis is analytical because it begins to answer HOW the artists reflected Renaissance values in their works—through "humanist techniques," "classical themes," and "secular realism."

C. (0 points) This is a simple restatement of the question.

D. (0 points) Although this statement does more than restate the question, it implies three very general categories of evidence without any explicit connection between these categories and the terms of the question. Additionally, these categories are particularly overused by students. Readers have seen the "social, political, and economic" divisions forced upon almost every question imaginable.

E. (1 point) This thesis makes essentially the same point as in Example A, except that this time there is an explicit connection between "Renaissance values" and "humanism, classicism, and individualism," and it alludes to three categories of evidence. Since it does not try to answer HOW the values are reflected in the works, it still lacks analysis, but the author might still establish these connections elsewhere in the opening paragraph or within the body of the essay.

F. **(1 point)** This is Example E with the addition of specific artists.

G. **(1 point)** The author has failed to explicitly identify "Michelangelo, Da Vinci, and Titian" as Italian artists of the Renaissance; however, in this instance it is unnecessary. These people are so famous that it may be assumed that this connection would be made by any reader. Additionally, unlike in Example A, here the author provides for the three distinct categories of evidence—the works of Michelangelo, those of Da Vinci, and those of Titian.

Analytical Thesis Development

In the exercise above, we alluded to the connection between an analytical thesis and the points for Analysis & Reasoning. *So what makes a thesis analytical anyway?* If you think of your thesis as the WHAT of your response, and your categories of evidence as the HOW of your response, then you can think of analysis as the WHY these categories matter to the thesis. After just this one sentence, the reader understands WHAT you intend to say, HOW you intend to say it, and WHY you have chosen to say it in this particular way. Yes, one sentence can do all that! That's a strong thesis.

So, once again, a strong essay begins with a strong thesis, and the strength of a thesis is determined by the ways in which it addresses the tasks and terms of the question. Once you have identified the tasks and terms of the question, brainstormed a list of essential evidence, and grouped your evidence into three logical categories, you are ready to develop an analytical thesis. To do this, you must decide how best to complete the tasks using the evidence available to you.

In the following example, the task is written as "to what extent." While it does not use a specific verb like most essay questions, this is still a common question format. Unfortunately, the misinterpretations of it are equally common. Many of the incorrect ways to answer this question include the phrase "to a great extent." The "to what extent" question is not asking "how much," but rather "how." The question may be rephrased as "in what ways is the relationship true and in what ways is it false?" The best answers should develop categories of evidence to demonstrate the truth of the relationship, and categories to show that it is false.

Exercise Question: *To what extent was Enlightenment thought rooted in the Scientific Revolution?*

Tasks: To what extent (In what ways is this true? AND In what ways is this false?)

Terms: Enlightenment thought, rooted, and Scientific Revolution

Question Restated: In what ways were Enlightenment ideas rooted in the Scientific Revolution? In what ways were Enlightenment ideas NOT rooted in the Scientific Revolution?

One way to complete this task is to identify specific Enlightenment ideas, and then to show whether or not those ideas are rooted in the Scientific Revolution. Below you can see a brief list of some Enlightenment ideas that you might have brainstormed in response to this question. Next to the list are some possible roots of each of these ideas. Those roots connected to the Scientific Revolution are identified with an (SR) after them.

Enlightenment Ideas	Roots
social contract	optimistic opinion of mankind, observation(SR) of British system, observation(SR) of French absolutism, Locke
capitalism	observation(SR) of mercantile policies
deism	new concepts of the universe(SR), Newton(SR), Galileo(SR), Descartes(SR)
natural law	Bacon(SR), observation(SR) of inequities of old regime

The challenge now is to make sense of the information in terms of the question. As you learned in Step 1, start to pose questions that link the terms with the question. When answering an "in what ways" or a "to what extent" question, it is often a good idea to categorize your evidence according to the "ways."

In what ways were Enlightenment ideas rooted in the Scientific Revolution?

- based on observation and analysis of observed evidence
- philosophers read and refer to ideas of specific SR thinkers (Newton, Galileo, Bacon, and Descartes)

In what ways were Enlightenment ideas NOT rooted in the Scientific Revolution?

- based on writings of Locke (not strictly SR)
- extrapolation from SR ideas to non-science conclusions is not supported by scientific method

So, the relationship is true in terms of "observation and analysis" and "the ideas of specific Scientific Revolution thinkers," but is false in terms of "unsupported extrapolation from SR ideas to non-science conclusions." It also appears to be false because some of the Enlightenment ideas derive from the writing of John Locke, who is of neither strictly the Enlightenment nor the Scientific Revolution. Since the other categories seem easier to develop using the evidence available, the sample thesis will ignore the Locke category.

Thesis: To the extent that the Enlightenment ideas of social contract, capitalism, and deism were based on a critical analysis of direct observations as well as on the writings of earlier scientists, they were rooted in the Scientific Revolution; however, to the extent that some of these Enlightenment social theories were extrapolated from scientific concepts without concrete rational justification, their development violated the spirit of the Scientific Revolution.

Guided Practice: Analytical Thesis Development

Directions: For each of the exercises in this set, follow the model you have learned to develop a thesis that answers the question. Be sure to complete each step of the prewriting process to insure that your response is well organized.

Step 1: Identify the tasks and terms

Step 2: Restate the question, and then create a chart to organize the ideas you brainstorm.

Finally, craft your analytical thesis statement.

> **Exercise Question:** Analyze the impact of the Ottoman expansion into Europe on European politics and society 1453–1600.

Explanation

Now compare your response to the sample response shown below. In order to be correct, your thesis does not need to be identical to the one that follows. Look for common characteristics that your thesis and the sample thesis share. Did you address the tasks fully? Did you include the terms? Did you organize your thesis around the HOW's or WHY's of the question? Did you imply clear categories of evidence?

Tasks: Analyze

Terms: Impact of the Ottoman expansion, European politics and society, 1453–1600

Question Restated: In what ways or for what reasons were European politics and society affected by the rise of the Ottomans between 1453 and 1600?

The web that follows is the result of brainstorming and organizing. At first, the details inside the white bubbles were just a list of evidence. As I began to look for logical groups, I developed the ideas in the black bubbles and grouped my brainstormed evidence accordingly. If you look at the resulting web, you can see that all the evidence connected with the fall of Constantinople helped to reinforce the Church split. The ongoing struggles between the West and the Ottomans in the period from Mehmet to Suleiman, meanwhile, led to the decline of the Venetians and the rise of the Hapsburgs.

Sample Chart:

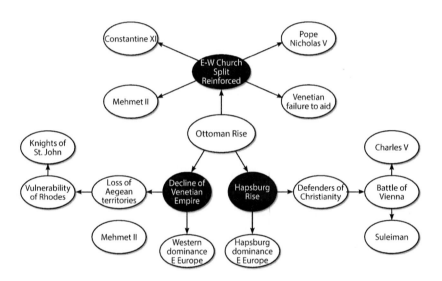

Compare the sample thesis with the web above.

Sample Thesis: The Ottoman expansion into Europe directly impacted European politics by elevating the Hapsburgs _who fought to repel them_ and diminishing the Venetians _who needed free access to the sea for trade_; and, by causing the fall of Constantinople, impacted European society through a heightened sense of mutual distrust _that helped to calcify the East-West split in the Christian churches_.

You should recognize each of the three categories of evidence as the ideas in the black bubbles around which the evidence is organized. The italicized phrases serve as analysis because they demonstrate why each category matters to this thesis. If your prewriting has produced something similar to the chart and thesis above, your essay is practically written for you.

Taking the Next Step

Remember, the structure of a thesis depends upon the categories of evidence that you have brainstormed. Review your answers for this section and take note of how you used those categories to construct your analytical thesis statements. Now you need to practice explaining the significance of those categories of evidence in your opening paragraph.

Writing the Opening Paragraph

For years, I've delivered a consistently harsh and loud message to my AP European History students. Whenever they would begin an essay with mounds of fluffy narrative that English teachers might call setting, I would cut them off at the knees with a sharp, "Answer the stinkin' question!" For 55 years the AP European History FRQ and DBQ rubrics rewarded clarity and directness—no points for setting. Students often get lost in their own text when they try to set the stage for an answer that even they don't fully understand yet, so banning setting altogether usually resulted in better—and higher scoring—essays. But now, some things have changed.

The newest AP European History LEQ and DBQ essay rubrics now reward setting—if you do it well. It is still a terrible idea to begin your essay with a page of directionless fluff that you hope will end in an acceptable thesis. A well-planned, purposeful setting that establishes the historical context of your argument, however, followed by a clear and direct answer to the question prompt, will definitely boost your score. More specifically, a thoughtful statement of setting at the start of your essay might be the best way to earn the point for Contextualization.

The Contextualization point is earned by explaining the broader context within which your argument is best understood. Sometimes this context is a series of events or an historical era, but it may also be an historical theme or process. In any case, situating your argument within its broader context is now a great idea when writing AP essays. And the best place to contextualize your argument is probably within the opening paragraph in the form of a well-structured setting.

So feel free to indulge your English teacher on the new AP European History essays, and create a few sentences that set the stage for your argument. Then... answer the stinkin' question!

Planning a Strong Opening

As with so many other components of good essays, there is really no absolutely correct way to develop your opening paragraph. Since clarity and directness are rewarded on both AP essay rubrics, we will develop a process that leads to a clear and direct opening paragraph.

For the sake of directness, don't spend too much space on setting in your essays. Although establishing the historical context for your answer is a great writing technique, too often students get lost in the setting and don't get to their thesis until page two. Instead, develop two to four sentences that can explain the historical "environment" within which your argument makes the most sense. Then write your thesis, and continue with your opening paragraph.

In the thesis, you addressed the tasks and terms of the question by stating explicitly WHAT you believe to be the answer to the question. You also outlined your three categories of evidence, which tell the reader HOW you intend to answer the question. If the thesis contains the answer to the question and all three categories of evidence, what are you going to write in the other sentences of the first paragraph? First, it should be noted that style and paragraph form are not assessed on the AP European History essay rubrics. So, if you write only the thesis in the opening paragraph, you will not be penalized. However, your essay will be well served if you develop your opening paragraph to state WHY your categories matter to your thesis—the same question you began to answer in your analytical thesis. One way to address this point is to write separate sentences for each category of evidence, answering briefly in each case, "Why does this matter to my thesis?"

Guided Practice: Presenting the Argument

Directions: For this set of exercises, you will practice all the skills covered so far in this book:

Step 1: Identify the tasks and terms

Step 2: Brainstorm specific evidence

Step 3: Develop a thesis and categories of evidence, and then outline your argument

Next, using the strategies outlined in the section above, write an opening paragraph for each thesis statement. The example below asks you to write an opening paragraph for the sample thesis shown, and is followed by a model solution to help you better understand the goal of this exercise.

> **Exercise Question:** Analyze the ways in which Italian Renaissance art reflects Renaissance values. Cite specific works and artists in your response.

Sample Thesis: Beginning in the 14th century, Italian artists, such as Michelangelo and Titian, reflected Renaissance values in their works through their use of humanist techniques, classical themes, and secular realism.

Explanation

Sample Opening Paragraph: Prior to the 14th century, artists devoted much of their work to the depiction of biblical scenes using highly symbolic imagery. Human characters in the were often anonymous foreground for the spiritual subjects. Artists spent little if any time attending to the physical traits of mere humans. Beginning in the 14th century, Italian artists, such as Michelangelo and Titian, reflected Renaissance values in their works through their use of humanist techniques, classical themes, and secular realism. Techniques, such as sculpting in the round, were reflective of Renaissance humanism, because they implied that man can understand his world. Classical themes of pagan mythology broke from the pre-Renaissance tradition of art focused on Christian subjects only. Finally, the use of realism in painting and sculpture utilized new techniques to focus on the human form rather than on Christian symbolism, as had been the practice before the Renaissance.

This opening begins with three brief sentences describing the artistic situation before the Renaissance. The setting quickly and purposefully establishes the value of our categories of evidence by highlighting the contrast between pre- and post-1300. In the thesis, we tell the reader that Michelangelo and Titian reflected Renaissance values in their works. We also say HOW the essay will illustrate this point—through humanist techniques, classical themes, and secular realism. Finally, in the subsequent sentences of the opening paragraph, we explain briefly WHY these three categories of evidence demonstrate Renaissance values. Some restatement of each of the sentences following the thesis could be used as topic sentences of each body paragraph, but we'll save that discussion for Step 5.

Taking the Next Step

Having completed your opening paragraph, you will have clearly told your reader WHAT you think is the answer to the question and HOW you will present the details of your argument. Once you've created this sturdy skeleton of an argument, now it's time to put some meat on the bones. In the next section, you will learn the best way to introduce specific evidence in the body of your essay, and how to best use that evidence in support of your thesis.

Writing the Body

I'm an idea guy—a big picture thinker. I happily go through each day brainstorming new and exciting ideas, often one after the next—some good, some not. Once, after a particularly rainy day at a campground, my friend, Bob (another idea guy), and I sat outside my RV with our feet in the mud, doing our best to enjoy the evening. Eventually, we both found ourselves staring across the road at a beat-up, old trailer with the intelligent addition of a small, wooden deck outside the front door. Meanwhile, there we sat, outside a brand new, fancy RV, with soaking wet shoes and muddy pant legs. Bob and I agreed that there was definitely a problem that needed to be addressed.

So that night we came up with a solution—a portable aluminum deck that we could disassemble and bring with us on all our RV camping trips. We were certain that it was a great idea, but we also understood that as long as it remained just an idea, we still had wet shoes. At some point, even idea guys have to get down to the work of fleshing out the details. So, we spent the next two years designing, testing, redesigning, and prototyping our solution. In the end, our idea became a reality—the Porta-Deck.

It's the same for your essay. By now you are likely very tired of all my harping on the benefits of thorough prewriting, and of course, it is your prewriting that allows you to more easily progress through the rest of the steps of writing a top-scoring AP European History LEQ or DBQ. But at some point in the process, your essay needs its details. It's time to get your feet out of the mud and write some body paragraphs.

Introduction to the Body Paragraph

In Step 2, we discussed evidence analysis as it applies to the prewriting phase of your essays. Now we have to address the writing phase. Even though your essay will benefit most from a clear argument and good organization—elements developed in your prewriting—you now have to actually write your essay.

Look back at the overview of the LEQ rubric guide on page 7 in Part 1 and you will see that—in order to earn even 1 of the 2 points in the Evidence section—you must support your thesis with *"specific* examples of *relevant* evidence." The inclusion of evidence is necessary, but not sufficient for the best LEQ responses. To earn the second Evidence point and have a chance at the top score, you have to explicitly analyze your evidence to "support" your thesis.

The easiest way to remember to analyze your evidence explicitly within the body of your essay is to continually ask yourself, "Why does this matter to my thesis?" Your answer to that question is the analysis required in your body paragraphs. Remember, as part of your prewriting, you developed categories of evidence—themes, concepts, and characteristics—that relate to the specifics of the essay question. Remember also that you used those categories of evidence to structure your thesis and, by extension, your essay as a whole. Now you are providing specific pieces of evidence that clarify or explain those categories. Every time you introduce new evidence, follow it with an explanation as to how it relates to that category of evidence. This will explain why it matters to your thesis.

Each body paragraph should be comprised of:

1. A topic sentence that states why this category of evidence matters to your thesis (Remember, your thesis is structured according to the categories of evidence you have chosen to answer the essay question.)

2. Sentences describing each specific piece of evidence (for example, a specific aspect of a time period or event)

3. Sentences analyzing why each piece of evidence develops a category of evidence, and therefore, matters to your thesis

If you have developed three categories of evidence—which should always be your goal—then you will end up with three body paragraphs. The following exercises are meant to use those skills for LEQs and DBQs.

Guided Practice: Analyzing Evidence for the Long Essay Question (LEQ)

Directions: For this set of exercises, you will practice all the skills covered so far in this book:

Step 1: Identify the tasks and terms

Step 2: Brainstorm specific evidence

Step 3: Develop a thesis and categories of evidence, and then outline your argument

Step 4: Write an opening paragraph.

Then, using your outline as a guide, write three body paragraphs, remembering that each time you introduce new evidence, you must also explicitly state why it matters to your thesis. Don't worry about writing style, transitions, or the closing—those things will be covered later in the book. Additionally, don't worry about timing and pacing. For now, it is more important to focus all of your attention on developing a written response that meets all the requirements of the AP LEQ rubric.

> *Exercise Question:* In what ways and for what reasons did art of the Renaissance outside of Italy differ from that of Italian Renaissance artists?

Explanation

Although you may have used different evidence and an entirely unique argument, look at the following explanation and check that you completed each step.

Tasks: In what ways AND for what reasons

Terms: Art, Renaissance outside Italy, Italian Renaissance artists

Categories of Evidence:

Italian Renaissance art portrayed biblical subjects

Renaissance art outside Italy had stronger Christian themes (Christian humanists)

Renaissance art outside Italy had stronger Christian themes (Protestant Reformation)

Sample Thesis: While Italian Renaissance art often portrayed biblical subjects, it tended to highlight the human aspects of those subjects, whereas Renaissance art outside of Italy had stronger Christian themes because of the influence of Christian humanists and the Protestant Reformation.

Sample Body Paragraph: The art of Michelangelo and Raphael typifies the style and subjects of Italian Renaissance art. Michelangelo became most famous for his sculptures and frescoes of biblical figures like Moses, Noah, and Adam and Eve. Raphael also painted biblical scenes like his Madonna of Seggiola. These Italian masters, like their compatriots, portrayed their subjects with an eye for realism, focusing on the humanity rather than the spirituality of their work. Each of these artists was equally well known, however, for his pagan subjects such as Venus, Zeus, and Bacchus, to name a few. Those artists of the Renaissance period outside of Italy, who portrayed subjects of Christianity, however, focused more on the spirituality of their subjects. Durer, for example, portrayed biblical images, like in *The Four Horsemen of the Apocalypse* and delved into the spiritual meanings behind his subject.

Review your response to the preceding exercise. The evidence that you provided was based upon information that you could recall from your previous work in European history. Did your evidence include any of the details in the sample above? You might want to check the list of Key Terms in the Appendix to see if there are other relevant details that could have been used with your argument.

Taking the Next Step

You've successfully written the body of an LEQ. The technique you used for evidence analysis in the LEQ works equally well in any thesis essay, so your hard work here will help you in college as well as on the AP exam. Now get ready, because next we will apply those new skills to body paragraphs in the DBQ.

In-body Document Analysis and Citation for the DBQ

The title of this section is long! However, to be totally descriptive, it would have to read "DBQ Document In-body Evidence and Critical Analysis and Methods of In-body Document Citation"—but that would be ridiculous. Basically, this section applies the skills you have just practiced in the previous section to DBQ essays.

For the DBQ, you will introduce and analyze documents included with the question, in addition to specific evidence that you can recall from your own study of European History. Just as with the LEQ, each time you introduce a new document or piece of specific evidence, you must explicitly state why it matters to your thesis. You will also include analysis of the document source at this time (see Step 2). Finally, each document should be cited within the body of your essay. If you have analyzed the source for a particular document, you will have already included a citation within the body of your essay. If not, you should still credit the source as it is noted in the document. Although explicit citation is not required by the rubric, you are required to use documents explicitly and individually, and citation is evidence of that use. In addition, when you write essays in your undergraduate classes, contextual citations demonstrate a mastery of the evidence and a sophistication of argument.

Here are a few examples of citations that might be found within successful DBQs citing the following document:

Document G

> **Source: Michelangelo Buonarroti, Italian Renaissance artist, letter to Giorgio Vasari, 1563**
>
> I have reached the twenty-fourth hour of my day, and... no project arises in my brain which hath not the figure of death graven upon it.

"According to Michelangelo, ..."

"As stated by Michelangelo Buonarroti in 1563, ..."

"Buonarroti, an Italian Renaissance artist, stated..."

"Document G says..."

"...(Doc G)"

"...(Michelangelo)"

"According to Michelangelo, ... (Doc G)"

Even though there is no particular format that earns greater credit from the readers, I encourage my students to use something similar to the last example. The parenthetical citation is redundant in this example, but it is a worthwhile redundancy. The contextual citation ("According to Michelangelo") is the most elegant way to note authorship in any kind of research assignment; however, it is not necessarily the most obvious at a glance. Although the AP Reader will spend several minutes reading your essay, and will definitely recognize a contextual citation as a valid reference to the document, if the reader, for any reason, finds it necessary to go back and quickly count the number of documents included in your essay, the parenthetical citation ("(Doc G)") is the most obvious. It only takes a moment longer to write, but it could mean the difference between a 7 and a 5.

While the most important part of any AP essay (LEQ or DBQ) is the thesis, 5 of the 7 possible points of the DBQ rubric are determined by the quality of your body paragraphs. To make certain that you score the points you need, always ask the following questions:

- Have you supported your thesis with six of the documents explicitly, individually, and correctly? **—2 points**
- Have you critically analyzed the source in at least three of the documents? **—1 point**
- Have you supported your thesis with at least one piece of specific evidence from outside the documents? **—1 point**
- Have you used your evidence to corroborate, qualify, or modify your argument? **—1 point**

A Note About Historical Complexity

"It's complicated, Dad." I hear this almost every day when talking with my 15-year-old daughter, Mia.

"How was school today?" I ask, believing the answer to be pretty straightforward.

"It's complicated, Dad."

"Is everything ok with your friends?"

"It's complicated, Dad."

"Any new boys in your life?"

"It's complicated, Dad."

Are there no easy answers? As a matter of fact, in life, as in history, there actually are no easy answers. If you find an easy answer, it's likely that you misunderstood the question.

Historical complexity is simply the recognition that there are no easy answers. In any historical argument, there will be evidence that corroborates, evidence that qualifies, and evidence that modifies the argument. Great essays account for and explain these corroborations, qualifications, and modifications. Here's an example from the French Revolution:

The Point: Women in the French Revolution achieved a high level of equality with men.

Corroborating Evidence:

- Condorcet argued for complete civil equality for women in 1789
- Women joined the Cercle Social to discuss women's rights in 1790
- Olympe de Gouges published Declaration of the Rights of Women in 1790
- Women formed the Society of Revolutionary Republican Women in 1793
- The French Republic referred to men and women as "citizens"

Qualifying Evidence:

- Women's clubs primarily focused on equality in marriage and education
- Most women participated in the revolution by supporting the efforts of their husbands
- The French words used for "citizen" are gender specific

Contradicting Evidence:

- Rousseau's writing, on which much of the revolution was based, specifically argued against women in the political sphere
- The Declaration of the Rights of Man and Citizen, a seminal work of the revolution, made no mention of women (a fact that motivated Olympe de Gouges to publish her declaration in 1790)
- Women's clubs were outlawed in 1793
- Olympe de Gouges was guillotined in 1793

- French women never gained the right to vote or hold office until 1944

It should be clear from this example that history is not black and white. Most historical arguments try to make sense of various shades of gray. That is the essence of historical complexity.

Guided Practice: Analyzing Evidence for the DBQ

Directions: For the following exercise, follow the process outlined in the preceding steps.

Step 1: Identify the tasks and terms

Step 2: Read and analyze the documents and brainstorm outside evidence (make notes in the margins)

Step 3: Develop a thesis and categories of evidence, and then outline your argument (grouping documents and outside evidence within your categories)

Step 4: Write an opening paragraph.

Then, using your outline as a guide, write three body paragraphs, remembering that each time you introduce a new document or piece of specific evidence, you must explicitly state why it matters to your thesis. Critically analyze the source wherever you can, and, for each document, develop the habit of combining a contextual citation with a sentence-ending parenthetical citation.

> ***Exercise Question:*** *To what extent was the Medici family responsible for the innovations of the Florentine Renaissance?*

Document A

SOURCE: **Filippo Brunelleschi, dome of Santa Maria del Fiore, Florence, 1446**

Document B

SOURCE: **Pope Leo X, Giovanni de Medici, on the naming of his godson in honor of his great-grandfather, 1519**

...[Cosimo was the] wisest, bravest, and most prudent man yet born to the house of Medici.

Document C

SOURCE: **Niccolo Machiavelli,** *History of Florence,* **1521–1525**

In peaceful times he [Lorenzo "the Magnificent" de Medici] often entertained the people with various festivities, such as jousts, feats of arms, and representations of triumphs of olden times. He aimed to maintain abundance in the city, to keep the people united and the nobility honoured. He had the greatest love and admiration for all who excelled in any art, and was a great patron of learning and of literary men, of which his conduct towards Cristofano Landini and Messer Demetrius the Greek furnishes the strongest proof.

Document D

SOURCE: **Benedetto Varchi,** *Storia Fiorentina* **[History of Florence], written 1540s**

That Greek letters were not completely forgotten, to the great loss of humanity, and that Latin letters have been revived to the infinite benefit of the people—this all Italy, nay all the world, owes to the high wisdom and friendliness of the house of the Medici.

Document E

SOURCE: **Giorgio Vasari,** *Lives of the Most Eminent Painters, Sculptors, and Architects,* **1550**

Of Filippo Brunellesco, it may be said that he was given by heaven to invest architecture with new forms, after it had wandered astray for many centuries.

Document F

SOURCE: **Giorgio Vasari,** *Lives of the Most Eminent Painters, Sculptors, and Architects,* **1550**

[Donatello] divined from the slightest indication all that Cosimo desired.

Document G

SOURCE: **Michelangelo Buonarroti, responding to his opportunity to surpass Brunelleschi's dome in Florence, circa 1563**

I will make a sister dome, larger, but not more beautiful.

Document H

SOURCE: **Giovanni Battista Cini, *Vita del Serenissimo Signor Cosimo I de' Medici primo granduca di Toscana*, 1611**

Cosimo [I] was by nature marvelously inclined to magnificence and to the beautification of all things.

Explanation

Although you may have used different evidence and an entirely unique argument, look at the following explanation and check that you completed each step.

Tasks: To what extent (In what ways AND In what ways NOT)

Terms: Medici family, innovations, Florentine Renaissance

Categories of Evidence:

Florentine artists were skilled and visionary

Artists needed money to produce their work

Medici were willing sponsors of art

Sample Thesis: To the extent that the artists of the Florentine Renaissance were skilled and visionary with or without sponsorship, the Medici were not directly responsible for the innovations of the period. Since the artists needed money to actually produce their greatest works, however, and since wealthy sponsors were rare, the Medici, as willing sponsors, must share some of the credit.

Sample Body Paragraph: If the money they spent supporting artists like Donatello, Brunelleschi, and Michelangelo were not evidence enough of the willingness of the Medici to sponsor great art, several contemporary authors will attest to the fact. Machiavelli wrote of Lorenzo the Magnificent's love of art and learning in his *History of Florence* (Document C). Of course, it is worth noting that the *History of Florence* was commissioned by Pope Leo X, Lorenzo's son, and that Machiavelli, formerly implicated in a plot to oust the Medici family, tried many times to redeem himself in their eyes. It is possible that he made all the Medici appear grander than they were in reality. However, both Varchi in his *History of Florence* (Document D) and Vasari in his *Lives of the Most Eminent Painters, Sculptors, and Architects* (Document F) corroborate Machiavelli's sentiments. Although it is possible that all three accounts were politically motivated, three separate sources attest to the Medici love of art and willingness to sponsor it.

Review the body paragraphs that you wrote for the preceding exercise. Make certain that, in each body paragraph, you have clearly demonstrated the relevance of your evidence in support of your thesis. As you have structured your thesis according to categories of evidence that respond to the terms of the essay question, so your paragraphs should move smoothly from one to the next, providing evidence that logically develops your thesis.

Taking the Next Step

Now that you've mastered each body paragraph, analyzing evidence and document sources, it's time to polish the spaces between your paragraphs with transition sentences. In the following section, you will learn how to provide effective transitions between your paragraphs and help your reader to follow the logic of your argument.

Transitions for Improved Analysis

Transitions make your essay sound better. Transitions help connect your ideas to each other. Transitions make your argument flow more smoothly. You should learn to use transitions. That's the point of this section of the book (without transitions).

Sounds a little choppy, right?

Now let's try to connect the ideas. Transitions make your essay sound better, but, more importantly, they help connect your ideas to each other. Since transition sentences can be used to explicitly connect the categories of evidence in your argument, they make your argument flow more smoothly. A smoother argument will sound much more persuasive, so you should learn to use transitions to improve the quality of your essays.

Better, right?

I'm sure your English teacher has given you a list of transition words that you should incorporate into your essays, such as "therefore," "however," "moreover," or "thus." At the root of this list is the idea that some words and phrases are very effective at joining separate-but-related, ideas. In a thesis essay, like the AP European History LEQ or DBQ, all the separate ideas are related to the thesis, so transitions are an appropriate means of connecting them. Although sometimes you will utilize your English teacher's list, more often, you will develop your transition sentences from the ideas themselves. The process is really very easy and, with practice, writing transitions will become second nature to you.

To create the best transitions, start with the logic of your argument. In Step 2, you practiced developing categories of evidence to support your thesis. In Step 3, you were encouraged to create analytical thesis statements by explicitly stating WHY or HOW your categories support your argument. Those WHYs and HOWs force you to assemble your categories of evidence in the most logical order to support your argument. Transition sentences simply reinforce this order. Look, for example, at the following question:

> **Example Question:** Compare and contrast the influence of nationalism on Italian and German unification.

An acceptable thesis might respond, "In both Italy and Germany, government officials, interested in unification for their own purposes, were able to use a popular spirit of nationalism to create unified kingdoms. German officials, however, were able to maintain control of this popular movement, whereas their Italian counterparts were barely able to keep up with the nationalist surge." Transition words in the thesis include *however* and *whereas*. These transitions are made possible by the order of our argument. Essentially, we're arguing that German and Italian unification were both assisted by nationalism, but in Germany the government effectively controlled the process while the nationalist movement in Italy surged ahead independent of the Italian government.

If we move on to the body of this essay, we'll see how these explicit statements of logic within our thesis serve as the foundation for the transitions between each paragraph. According to the order we've established in this thesis, the first body paragraph should analyze evidence demonstrating the ways in which the German and Italian governments utilized nationalism to further their goals of unification. The second body paragraph will detail how and why German officials retained control of the nationalist movement, while the third body paragraph will analyze the evidence that demonstrates the Italian government's lack of control over the same movement in its own states.

No matter what details you decide to include in these paragraphs, the transition between the first two body paragraphs could read, "Despite the similarities in outcomes for Germany and Italy, the process for each country was very different." We can reinforce these differences with a transition between the second and third body paragraphs that says, "Whereas Germany was able to use—and even to co-opt—the nationalist spirit within its territories, Italian nationalism tended to work independently of (if not counter to) the goals of Piedmont's officials and became a force that required great energy to control." Essentially, these two sentences do the same thing as "however" and "whereas" in the opening paragraph.

I hope you can see that transition sentences, as used above, make the logic of your argument more explicit to the reader. Your essay may be good without them, but it will be fantastic with them. As you proceed through the rest of this book, try to develop the habit of adding a sentence at the end of each body paragraph that serves to explicitly connect your main ideas and make your argument flow more smoothly. You can begin developing that habit with the exercise that follows.

Guided Practice: Analytical Transitions

Directions: For the following exercise, you will continue to practice all the skills covered so far in this book:

Step 1: Identify the tasks and terms

Step 2: Brainstorm specific evidence (and analyze the documents in the DBQ)

Step 3: Develop a thesis and categories of evidence, and then outline your argument

Step 4: Write an opening paragraph

Step 5: Analyze your specific evidence in three body paragraphs

Now, using the example above as a model, write a transition sentence between the first and second body paragraph and another one between the second and third. Your transitions should connect the main ideas of your argument. Remember that transitions are not simply exercises in good writing style, but can reinforce the logic of your argument for the reader.

> **Exercise Question:** In what ways did the papacy help to determine the direction of the Italian Renaissance in the 15th and 16th centuries?

Explanation

Sample Thesis: The papacy helped to determine the direction of the Italian Renaissance through its control of education, its patronage of the arts, and its ambitious building plans for the Vatican.

Sample Transition: *(insert between the second and third body paragraphs)* While the popes of the 15th and 16th centuries probably would have sponsored many works of art anyway, it was the ambitious plans for rebuilding the Vatican that presented the greatest reason for such sponsorship.

Taking the Next Step

At this point, you have mastered every part of the essay that earns points on the AP rubrics. But there is still one more piece of the puzzle—the closing paragraph. Although seemingly "pointless" (according to the rubrics), the final paragraph of your essay may hold the key to your ultimate success.

Step 5 Writing the Body

Sticking the Landing
—The Closing Paragraph

In 1996 the U.S. Women's Gymnastics Team won the gold medal, but the team's ultimate fate came down to the final competitor in the final event. As Team USA entered its final event, vaulting, the NBC commentators were giddy with excitement because the girls already had a commanding lead over the Russians and it certainly seemed like a lock. But then, the unthinkable happened. Jaycie Phelps started the event with an aerial feat so unique and spectacular that it bears her name—The Phelps. Every muscle in her 16-year-old legs flexed to power her down the runway toward the horse. She leapt into the air, propelled her body skyward off the horse, twisting and tumbling with such speed that it was nearly impossible to recount the entire routine. But, just as she spun into her blind landing, the forward momentum of her body as her feet hit the ground forced her to take a short hop before coming to a complete stop. The crowd gasped, and her parents dropped their heads into their hands in disbelief. That hop cost Jaycie and her team at least one-tenth of a point, and her final score of 9.662 opened a door for the Russian team to move up.

A series of similarly flawed vaults, including three falls in a row, left the fate of Team USA in the hands of young Kerri Strug. Under normal conditions, Kerri would be a good bet. But in this instance, because of the mistakes of her teammates, she needed an almost perfect 9.7 to win the gold for her team. Additionally, she had fallen on her first attempt, spraining her ankle and earning only a 9.162.

So now, after limping back to the start of the runway, Kerri Strug had to complete a one-and-a-half twist and land it with perfection on only one strong leg. At this point, the TV commentators were voicing the concerns of every distraught U.S. fan watching the event. Kerri gathered herself, raced down the runway—her ankle already throbbing—hit the horse and sprung into the air, and in an unbelievable demonstration of courage, Kerri Strug *stuck the landing*—picture perfect. The crowd erupted with excitement, and Team USA won the gold! The force of that landing damaged Kerri's ankle even further and, amid the applause, she fell to the ground and needed help to get back to her team. Kerri's score? 9.712—all because she stuck the landing!

Lasting Impressions

Fortunately, the AP essays are not much like Olympic gymnastics. If you do everything right in the opening and body of your essay, the closing paragraph doesn't really matter to your score. In fact, according to the rubrics, you don't even need a closing paragraph. So why even include this section in the book? Because your closing paragraph is, in fact, similar to Olympic gymnastics in one crucial way—the applause. As you've read earlier, the AP essays are not machine-scored. Real people read the essays and apply the AP standards to determine the scores. A strong closing paragraph restates your thesis, recounts your argument, and reminds the Reader about your best evidence and exactly why you deserve the top score!

The best part is that writing a great closing paragraph is way easier than sticking the landing at the end of the vault. In fact, you already did most of the heavy lifting when you wrote your opening paragraph. Just like the opening, your closing paragraph should include statements explaining the importance of each of your categories of evidence and a restatement of your thesis. Unlike your opening, the category statements within your closing paragraph should allude to the best evidence from the body of your essay.

So, what can you do to insure that your closing paragraph is more than just a dull restatement of your opening—a misstep on the landing? Begin with the reason you are writing the closing in the first place: the applause. You need to show your reader, in one final magnificent ta-da, that your argument is worth every bit of a 7 on the DBQ rubric (6 on the LEQ rubric). Review the logical steps of your argument one category at a time, and each time you state one of these generalizations, allude to that category's strongest piece of specific evidence for illustration. Then, after you've refreshed your categories of evidence, use the momentum of this powerful reformulation of your argument to clearly restate your thesis. All that will remain to be done is to catch your breath, stand up straight, raise your arms, and bask in the glory of victory.

Need further clarification? Let's look at an example. In this question, you are asked to, "Describe and analyze the components of the Catholic Reformation in Spain." Here is one example of an opening paragraph:

Sample Opening Paragraph: Among the components of the Catholic Reformation in Spain were the Jesuits, who worked through education and conversion; the Inquisition, which operated through fear; and the monarchy, which used conquest and royal edict to conduct Reformation activities. While the Society of Jesus reached out to find new converts and teach them the ways of Christianity, the Dominicans sought to root out heretics from within. With the support of the Spanish monarchy, these two religious orders expanded and cleansed the ranks of the faithful in Spain.

Although you haven't been asked to write an entire essay, you might have envisioned some very good, specific evidence to follow this opening paragraph. For instance, you may have considered that Pope Paul III authorized Ignatius Loyola's Society of Jesus largely because, by 1540, the Roman Catholic Church was being drained of its followers by Protestantism. Loyola and the Jesuits attacked the problem directly through Catholic teaching in Protestant territories, and indirectly through missionary Christianizing in Asia and the Americas. In the second body paragraph, you could have mentioned the infamous Grand Inquisitor of Spain, Tomás de Toquemada. As a Dominican priest, accustomed to strict discipline and extreme sacrifice, he was particularly well-suited to enforcing the laws of the Church and prosecuting heretics. Although Toquemada predates the Reformation period, you might have used him as the model for future inquisitors. Finally, in your third body paragraph, you likely would have analyzed the religious roots of the battles of the Spanish

Armada. Perhaps you would have included evidence of the Catholic conquest of Granada and the expulsion of the Jews in 1492—just prior to the start of the Reformation period. There is much to support the argument that the Reconquista demonstrated a Spanish commitment to vigorous defense of the Catholic faith.

For the Jesuits, we need to remind the reader that they led the charge to fill—and refill—the ranks of the Catholic faithful. Paul III's original motivations in authorizing the new order may be the perfect evidence to support that contention. We mentioned the Dominicans in the opening paragraph as a part of the Inquisition, so Spain's first Grand Inquisitor is an excellent bit of evidence to hammer home in the closing. The Spanish crown, more so than any other monarchy of its time, institutionalized the Catholic Reformation within its borders. Philip's use of the armada against Elizabeth's Protestant England serves as an ideal illustration of that point. The following closing paragraph will state each of these points and conclude with a slightly reformulated thesis.

> **Sample Closing Paragraph:** Pope Paul III understood fully the Church's need to replenish its ranks, and the Jesuits met that need by converting new Catholics in Europe and abroad. As the Society of Jesus was the perfect missionary order, so were the Dominicans perfect for the Inquisition. Tomás de Toquemada combined evangelism and terror to bring order to the Catholic faith in Spain. His success, and, later, that of the Jesuits, was assisted by the work of Catholic monarchs like Philip II. Although the Spanish Armada failed in its attempt to squash the upstart Protestant queen of England, it demonstrates Spain's commitment to the Catholic faith. Through religious education, coercion, and royal conquest, the Jesuits, the Inquisition, and the monarchy became the key components of the Catholic Reformation in Spain.

That's it. This paragraph summarizes the argument and drives home the thesis.

Here is one final note about closing paragraphs. **Never introduce new arguments at the end of the essay.** This is especially true for evaluative arguments—statements that preach a moral—but is equally true for statements attempting to earn Synthesis credit by expanding the argument. Although these closing statements will not hurt you on the rubric, remember that the closing paragraph is largely for effect. New arguments tend to distract the reader from the point you were attempting to drive home. Many well-meaning—but misguided—students may have ended the example paragraph above with, "Since conquest and torture are not Christian ideals, it is clear that the Catholic Reformation was not very 'Christian.'" This final statement, suddenly attempting to contrast Christian ideals with the Catholic Reformation, could be as damaging to the overall effect of the essay as a gymnast's belly-flop onto the mat.

Guided Practice: Effective Closing Paragraphs

Directions: For the following exercise, practice all the skills covered so far in this book.

Step 1: Identify the tasks and terms

Step 2: Analyze the documents and brainstorm specific evidence

Step 3: Develop a thesis and categories of evidence, and then outline your argument

Step 4: Write an opening paragraph

Step 5: Analyze your specific evidence in three body paragraphs and insert analytical transitions

Then, using the example shown above in this section ("Catholic Reformation in Spain") as a guide, write a closing paragraph for your essay. Remember that this final paragraph is your best opportunity to "stick the landing" in your essay. Summarize each part of your argument, alluding to your most significant evidence, and restate your thesis—ta-da!

> **Exercise Question:** Analyze the connection between peace and financial success in Venice in the 15th and 16th centuries.

Document A

SOURCE: **Tommaso Mocenigo, Doge of Venice, on joining Florence in war against Milan, February 1422**

In our time, we have seen Giovanni-Galeazzo, Duke of Milan, who conquered all Lombardy, save Florence, the Romagna, and the Campagna di Roma, reduced to such straits by his expenses that he was obliged to remain quiet during five years; and it was with much ado then that he paid his troops. So it happens to all. If you preserve peace, you will amass so much money, that all the world will hold you in awe. My Lords, you see how, year by year, in consequence of the troubles of Italy, families migrate hither, and help to swell our population. If the Florentines give themselves to the Duke, so much the worse for them who interfere! Justice is with us. They have spent everything, and are in debt. We have a capital of 10,000,000, on which we gain 4,000,000. Live in peace, fear nothing, and trust not the Florentines! ... We wage battle against the Infidels only; and great are the praise and glory which we reap. So long as I live, my Lords, I will maintain those principles which I have hitherto followed, and which consist in living at peace!

Document B

SOURCE: **Tommaso Mocenigo, Doge of Venice, on his deathbed, 1422**

Our City at present sends abroad for purposes of trade in various parts of the world 10,000,000 ducats a year, of which the interest is not less than 2,000,000. ... We find 1,000 gentlemen with means varying between 700 and 4,000 ducats a year. If you continue to prosper in this manner, you will become masters of all the gold in Christendom. But, I beseech you, keep your fingers from your neighbours, as you would keep them out of the fire, and engage in no unjust wars: for in such errors God will not support princes!

Document C

SOURCE: **Pietro Orio, speaking against the election of Francesco Foscari as Doge, April 1423**

...if he was made Doge, Venice would be perpetually at war.

Document D

SOURCE: **Francesco Foscari, Doge of Venice, speaking of war with Milan, December 3, 1425**

Carmagnola's [Francesco Bussone, Count of Carmagnola] speech has laid before you the power and the resources of Filippo [Filippo Visconti of Milan]. They are not so great as rumour has represented them. Nor should we be justified in looking for any other than a happy and prosperous conclusion to our enterprise under Carmagnola as the captain of our arms. For he is versed in war; nor can all Italy show his equal this day in bravery and proficiency in the military art. Under such a general is offered us, beyond all doubt, the certain hope of extending our borders. All these considerations urge us to undertake the war with a good courage; a war, I repeat, which is necessary; for our enemy is powerful, neighbor to us, and aspires to the sovereignty of Italy. Let us embark upon this war, then, and avenge our wrongs by trampling in the dust our common foe, to the everlasting peace of Italy.

Document E

SOURCE: **Giulio Porro, Venetian chronicler, on Milan's attack on the Venetian fleet, 1431**

...[Paolo Correr] on hearing the guns and seeing the ducal galleons bearing down, told Carmagnola that he ought either to attack Cremona (by way of causing a diversion) or to march down to the banks of the Po to support the doge's fleet, which had come up the river on his orders... .

Document F

> **SOURCE: Philippe de Comines, French ambassador to Venice, 1495**
>
> [Venice is] the most triumphant city that I have ever seen. ...impossible to describe the beauty, magnificence, and wealth. ...[the Grand Canal is] the most beautiful street in the world.

Document G

> **SOURCE: Marin Sanudo, Venetian patrician, in an essay on the origins of Venice, 1493**
>
> The city is about 7 miles in circumference; it has no surrounding walls, no gates which are locked at night, no sentry keeping watch as other cities have for fear of enemies; it is so very safe at present, that no one can attack or frighten it. As another writer said, its name has achieved such dignity and renown that it is fair to say Venice merits the title "Pillar of Italy," "deservedly it may be called the bosom of all Christendom."

Explanation

Sample Thesis: In Venice of the 15th and 16th centuries, peace was associated with economic prosperity, while war was generally associated with economic instability, except when the war was viewed as justified.

Sample Closing Paragraph: The Venetian view of peace and war is best exemplified by the words of the doge Tommaso Mocenigo who warned his people to, "engage in no unjust wars." The economic success of Venice had been built on her ability to stay out of the fray, and engage in commerce with all parties. Venetians would enter into war only with a just cause, like the defense of Christianity. They were so devoted to peace that Francesco Foscari, appealing for war with Milan, said that it would bring "everlasting peace to Italy." Throughout the 15th and 16th centuries, Venetians saw peace as the path to economic prosperity and war as the way to economic instability, except when the war was justified.

Taking the Next Step

Ta-da! You have stuck the landing! Review your conclusions and note how they flow organically from the logic of your paper. Pay attention to any techniques you used to move your readers smoothly out of your essay, without raising new issues or topics.

By now, you have learned—and hopefully mastered—the process of writing LEQ and DBQ essays. Note how writing a conclusion fits into that process. Now it is time to think about how you can accomplish that process within the time frame provided for the exam.

Preparing for the Exam

Beating the Clock

In my class, I spend most of the year trying to convince students to stop worrying about how long it takes them to answer the essay questions. "Focus on perfecting the process" is what I say; "worry about time and pacing later." Of course, on that one day in May, time matters, so you have to worry about it at some point. The problem with obsessing about time too soon is that it leads to bad habits. Writers who are worried about time omit some of their prewriting and often do a too-hasty job of brainstorming evidence. They erroneously believe that the solution to the time problem is writing from the moment the test booklet lands on the desk. This approach completely ignores everything we've discussed and practiced on the last 80+ pages. Remember, the rubrics reward good planning.

The real answer to improving your time on the essays is writing more essays. If you play a musical instrument, you likely learned to play the notes slowly. Speed came naturally as your skill improved. That's exactly what needs to happen with your essays. Master the steps of the writing process slowly at first, and then practice until your speed improves. *Mastering the Essay* provides plenty of practice for both LEQ and DBQ essays. In fact, if you have worked through each and every section, completing the practice exercises along the way, you are probably wondering why this section even exists. The practice exams in the Exercise Workbook are included to provide you with an opportunity (actually, three opportunities) to simulate the actual AP European History exam conditions. Each exercise requires that you write two essays (a DBQ and an LEQ), under the same time constraints imposed on the May exam. Furthermore, each of your LEQs must be chosen from among three questions, just like on the actual exam. Although this process may seem inconsequential, for some students the choice poses a significant barrier to their success.

Choosing an LEQ

There are many philosophies regarding the choice of an LEQ question, and many teachers will share their own theories with their students. Ultimately, there is no technique that is necessarily better than the rest. However, no matter what your method of decision-making, a few key points should be considered.

1. You must feel relatively comfortable with the terms of the question.

2. You must completely understand the tasks demanded in the question.

3. You must choose quickly, because the rubric offers no reward for your decision.

4. Every question will be assessed according to the same general standards, so there is no inherently better question.

5. Be very wary of a question that seems much easier than the other. Students often misread the tasks, which can lead to a partially off-topic response.

In the end, your choice must depend more on your understanding of history than on some strategy to outsmart the test-makers. As soon as you have finished writing your DBQ, move to the LEQ group, carefully read each question, quickly choose the one you would like to answer, and begin your pre-writing process. The choice should take you no more than a minute or two.

The test-makers recommend that you devote 45 minutes (after the 15-minute reading period) to the DBQ and 30 minutes to the LEQ. This is a good rule of thumb and, although the times are not required, you should make every attempt to follow these guidelines. As stated earlier in the book, it is quite normal for students to use more than 15 minutes for the DBQ prewriting, but since prewriting actually helps to shorten your writing time, you should still aim to finish writing the DBQ by the end of the first hour of the essay section of the exam.

You should never find yourself approaching the final essay with fewer than 20 minutes remaining. But, what if something extraordinary happens—sudden illness, loss of memory, asteroid falls to Earth—and you run out of time in the middle of writing your final essay? In this very unlikely event, you should write as much as you can until the final minute of the testing period. Then list all of your remaining evidence (from your brainstorming notes—never omit the prewriting steps) so the reader will be able to see that you knew what should have been included. If you have already written enough to demonstrate a good grasp of the tasks and terms of the question, this list might help. Of course, if you have followed all the steps recommended in this book, and you have completed all of the exercises, you will not need this last piece of advice.

Use the practice exams to develop a sense of good pacing. A great practice technique is to use a stopwatch to time each portion of the test. After you finish a practice test, review the times you spent on each of the essays and, if necessary, adjust your pacing on the next test. By the time you have completed all three practice tests, you will feel very confident about your performance on the upcoming AP European History exam.

Part 3

The Other Question Types

The New AP Multiple-Choice

Every September for 33 years, I entered my classroom for the first time... again. And for most of those years, the class I anticipated more enthusiastically than any other was AP European History. I love the stories of European history. I love the spirit of high school seniors willing to take on the challenge of an AP class. I love the personal challenge of trying to guide those seniors through a complicated chronology coupled with college-level writing skills until they can achieve the ultimate goal—a 5 on the AP Euro exam.

You know what I don't love? The one question that is asked every year, and every year it grates on my nerves:

"What's a good AP prep book?"

By "good," they mean chock full of little factoids they can cram to prepare for the Multiple-Choice section of the exam.

For years, I've responded with my standard, "They all stink! If you want history content, read the textbook and stay awake in class. If you want to do well on the AP exam, learn to write like a college freshman, because writing is what matters most on the AP exam." And every year, my students give me a polite nod and then go out and buy one, two, and sometimes three AP prep books.

So why am I so against the run-of-the-mill prep book? Because it is basically an outline of European history, thrown together by some big-box publisher who preys on the deepest fear expressed by most AP European History students—that they don't know or haven't memorized enough details for the MC section of the exam.

The reality is that nobody knows enough. **Most of the smartest kids in the country barely get half of the multiple-choice questions correct.**[1] So how do they get those 4s and 5s? Writing. Great essays add up to great scores.

But...

Since you will spend almost an hour answering multiple-choice questions on the exam, you might as well do the best you can. So let's take a look at the multiple-choice question format.

The New Format

On the AP exam, multiple-choice questions appear in sets of 2-5 questions based on a single document prompt. The document prompts might be excerpts from primary sources or secondary sources, charts, graphs, maps, or images.

The questions are designed in a way that makes them difficult (if not impossible) to answer with only the document, and equally difficult to answer with only your knowledge of history. **The questions require you to combine your analysis of the document with your understanding of history.**

Here's an example:

Questions 1–3 refer to the passage below.

"Wretched Romans [citizens of Constantinople], how you have been led astray! You have departed from hope, which rests in God, by trusting in the power of the Franks [Western Europeans]. As well as the City itself, which will soon be destroyed, you have lost the true religion... Be aware, miserable citizens, what you are doing today... you have denied the true faith handed down to you by your forefathers. You have confessed your impiety. Woe to you when you are judged!"

Gennadios (formerly Georgios Scholarios), Byzantine monk, in a manifesto against union with the Western Church, November 1, 1452

1. The passage illustrates the tensions generated by which of the following historical events?

   A. The Great Schism between the Eastern and Western Christians

   B. The impending threat of an Ottoman assault on Constantinople

   C. The posting of Martin Luther's 95 Theses

   D. The Venetian attack on Constantinople in the Fourth Crusade

2. Which of the following was most directly caused by the crisis associated with the passage?

   A. The Protestant Reformation

   B. The War of Spanish Succession

   C. The Italian Renaissance

   D. The First World War

3. Gennadios' criticisms are most similar to those of which of the following?

   A. Charles de Gaulle and his followers upon the surrender of France in 1940

   B. Martin Luther at the Diet of Worms

   C. The Council of Trent regarding the Protestant revolt

   D. The defenders of Verdun in the First World War

As you can see, these ain't your father's multiple-choice questions! However, they do share several characteristics with previous multiple-choice questions from way back when. Most important among those characteristics is that you need not generate an answer from out of the blue—the correct response is right in front of you. Also, like earlier multiple-choice questions, the wrong answers are

---

1 – http://research.collegeboard.org/programs/ap/data

often designed specifically to serve as distracters—that is, they have elements of truth that might seem to relate to the topic but do not specifically answer the question. The differences between these new MC questions and their predecessors, however, are striking.

As stated earlier, it is nearly impossible to answer the questions without BOTH analyzing the document in the prompt, AND remembering specific details from history. In this way, the test-makers hope to evaluate your understanding of history, as well as your historical thinking skills. Also, you may have noticed that each question includes only four answer choices—no more choice E. Along with the fifth choice, the test-makers have also eliminated the wrong answer penalty, so **answering every question, no matter what, is your best tactic**.

So let's see how well you did with the example questions.

Analyzing the Document

First, you needed to analyze the document prompt. Remember the **3-Step Process**? It works for MC questions on the new exam.

❶ **Summarize:** *What does the document say?*

It says that the citizens of Constantinople have abandoned their trust in God and instead put their faith in the Westerners. It implies that this is a mistake that will cause the downfall of Constantinople and the damnation of its citizens.

❷ **Analyze:** *Why does it matter?*

The document highlights the tensions among the people of the Roman Empire (Byzantines) in the mid-15th century. Among these stresses are the differences they have with the Roman Catholic Church of the West and the survival of the city of Constantinople.

❸ **Criticize:** *How might the source have influenced the meaning of the document?*

As a Byzantine monk, Gennadios is likely a strict adherent to the beliefs of the Eastern Orthodox Church, which by 1452, would be in stark contrast to those of the Roman Catholics. Consequently, his rabid attacks on the "Franks" (a pejorative term used to describe Western Europeans) might be a product of his own longstanding hatred of Roman Catholicism as much as any immediate crisis.

Next, it's time to answer the questions.

Analyzing the Answer Choices

Q1 - Contextualization

Question 1 is the easiest of the three because it simply requires an understanding of the basic historical context of the prompt. **Contextualization** is an important historical thinking skill, and one that will be assessed again and again on the new AP European History MC section. In this case, the relevant information is that Gennadios is worried about the well-being of the Byzantines and the document was written in 1452.

You should remember from your history class that the city of Constantinople fell to the Ottomans in 1453, so it could be that the stress in Gennadios' language is inspired by the threat of the Ottoman attack on the city—answer choice B. Notice that incorrect answers A and C allude to religious conflicts, which may seem connected to Gennadios' discussion of faith, but neither of which answers the question. Answer choice D is interesting because it discusses an event that preceded the document by 300 years, but with which you might be unfamiliar. It's an old-school MC question trick—"I don't know the answer to this question AND I don't know what this answer says, so, therefore, this answer must be correct." Not so. Don't fall for it.

Q2 - Causation

Causation is another important historical thinking skill that will be assessed many times in the multiple-choice section of the exam. Question 2 asks you to connect the crisis (the Fall of Constantinople) with some future effect of that crisis. Historians list several effects of the Ottoman conquest of Constantinople, and among them is the acceleration of the Italian Renaissance caused by the rapid influx of ancient Greek and Roman writings brought to Italy by Byzantine scholars escaping the Ottoman onslaught.

These "new" ideas helped to fuel an already smoldering humanism in Italy—answer choice C. Like in Q1, answer choice A harkens to the religious nature of the document. Answer D is somewhat more insidious because, if you know the connection at all, you might associate the rise of the Ottomans in 1453 with the fall of the Ottomans in WWI. The two are loosely connected but not necessarily cause-and-effect, and certainly not as directly causal as Constantinople and the Renaissance. Finally, choice B is another left-field response—it has no connection and is there simply to distract students who have little or no memory of the events of 1453.

Q3 - Comparison

Comparison, especially across time, is also assessed on the new MC section of the AP exam. Question 3 requires you to distill the essence of Gennadios' argument and to compare that with the argument of another historical actor in another historical period. Essentially, Gennadios is saying that the Byzantines have abandoned their own principles in favor of an antithetical position because they wish to save themselves in the moment. It is clear from the document that he believes they have now lost both their principles and their city.

This sounds very much like the argument made by Charles de Gaulle and the Free French after Marshal Petain surrendered to the Nazis in 1940. De Gaulle and his followers believed that the Vichy government had sacrificed its principles for a false peace with Hitler—answer choice A. Answers B and C both conjure the religious nature of the document and answer choice D is another choice from out of the blue.

Short-Answer Questions

If you've ever seen the movie *Stand by Me*, you may remember the scene when Gordie ponders, "Mickey's a mouse, Donald's a duck, Pluto's a dog. What's Goofy?" This random question leaves the four best friends baffled as they try, but fail, to reason out the Disney character's true species.

Little did they know that even Art Babbitt, the Disney animator who created Goofy, had trouble defining the character. "Think of the Goof as a composite of an everlasting optimist, a gullible Good Samaritan, a half-wit..." wrote Babbitt in 1934. He conceded "a vague similarity" between Goofy and Pluto, but insisted that their animation made them "entirely different... One is dog. The other human." So what is Goofy?

Now, the Disney Corporation declares him to be a dog, but I'm not entirely sure that will settle the issue. After all, Disney's other dog, Pluto, wears only a collar, walks on all fours and even barks—he is definitely a dog. By contrast, Goofy is always featured in pants and a shirt, he always walks completely upright, and speaks in English—he never barks. Furthermore, he clearly has hands and feet—no paws. Disney may want to redefine Goofy, but if you wear your underwear on your head, can you really call it a hat?

The Hybrid Question

This is the issue with the newest member of the AP European History exam—the Short-Answer Question (SAQ). The College Board® has declared this to be a hybrid question format. It is neither a writing question nor strictly an objective question. Like the new Multiple-Choice Questions, the SAQs often begin with a document prompt, but then students are required to generate their own answers without any given choices. Sounds like a short essay, but the scoring criteria make the two open-ended question types "entirely different."

According to the College Board®, students need not formulate paragraphs or thesis statements in their responses. Bulleted answers are encouraged. So, the SAQ is neither essay nor MC; it is, in fact, an entirely new breed of AP question, and one you will need to be prepared to tackle.

Since you must generate your responses from scratch, thinking of the SAQ as a writing exercise can be most useful. You may not need to respond with a thesis, but as I am fond of saying in class, everything is a thesis. So treating this as a thesis exercise will not hurt you. The SAQ rubric requires you to make explicit connections within your answer, which sounds like analysis. So our approach will resemble that of the LEQ without the stress of worrying about form and style. Let's take a look at a couple of examples.

1. Use the passage below and your knowledge of European history to answer all parts of the question that follows.

> "Whether or not Catherine de' Medici, Henry VIII, and the Turkish Sultans truly took their inspiration from *The Prince*, Machiavelli has suffered, more grievously than any other author, from guilt by association. Lorenzo di Piero de' Medici may have spurned the book in 1516, but few dictators or tyrants since then have neglected its lessons. Oliver Cromwell owned a manuscript copy; a well-thumbed edition accompanied Napoleon Bonaparte to the Battle of Waterloo; and Adolf Hitler admitted to keeping a copy on his bedside table."

> *Ross King,* Machiavelli: Philosopher of Power, *published 2007*

A. Provide one piece of evidence that supports King's contention about Machiavelli in the passage.

B. Provide one piece of evidence that undermines King's contention about Machiavelli in the passage.

C. Identify one example of any other author whose writings may
    have impacted his or her reputation in the way described by
    King.

Like all SAQs, Question 1 is divided into three parts, all based on
the original prompt. In this case, the prompt is a secondary source
document. The prompt may be a primary source document, map,
chart, graph, or image—or it might include no document at all (see
the next example).

In Question 1 you are asked to read the document and provide
evidence—first in support of the argument, then in opposition. Then,
in Part C, you are required to identify a parallel example from some
other context. Since this SAQ is based on a document, let's begin with
document analysis.

Anaylzing the Document

Once again, the 3-Step Process:

❶ **Summarize:** *What does the document say?*

The author suggests that Machiavelli's reputation was tarnished
by association, because of the list of historical bad guys who may
have taken their inspiration from *The Prince*.

❷ **Analyze:** *Why does it matter?*

Machiavelli's notoriety as a cynic is based largely on his
statement about how "the ends justify the means," and history
has provided countless examples of evil acts done in the name
of "honorable" goals. If Machiavelli did not actually share the
opinions of his admirers, maybe he is not such a bad guy.

❸ **Criticize:** *How might the source have influenced the meaning of the document?*

This 2007 biography by Ross King is subtitled *Philosopher of Power*. The positive tone of this subtitle seems to indicate that King views Machiavelli favorably. This document might actually summarize King's entire thesis.

Explanation

So now onto the answers.

Part A asks for evidence that might support King's contention that Machiavelli earned his "bad guy" rep from his association with bad guys who used his words. If you know anything about Machiavelli from class, you might remember that he was a Florentine diplomat. As a young man, he earned a reputation as a person who had the skills to negotiate and compromise to avoid conflict. Any of this information might be explained in such a way that it could help to support King's thesis.

Part B requires evidence to the contrary. Again, you may remember that Machiavelli wrote *The Prince* in order to win favor with the ruling family in Florence. Even if he didn't believe that "the ends justify the means," he wrote those words for the sake of winning a better position.

Finally, **Part C** asks you to identify another author whose reputation was influenced by his/her writing. This one seems very difficult, but couldn't you argue that the reputation of any author is based primarily on the words that person has written? With that in mind, choose another famous author and make that argument. Isaac Newton, for instance, is renowned for his scientific writings. His reputation has been elevated by the many scientists who have built upon the foundations of Newton's Laws. But you may know from history that Newton was actually quite a villain in his day. He was tyrannical, spiteful, and paranoid—not the type of person we would associate with true greatness.

Now that you understand the basic approach, here is another example of an SAQ. This one has no document and the three parts are divided very differently. Check it out.

2. Answer all parts of the question.

Historians have argued that the Renaissance was not really a "rebirth" of European civilization, but rather a continuation of medieval culture.

A. Identify TWO pieces of evidence that support this argument and explain how each supports the argument.

B. Identify ONE piece of evidence that undermines this argument and explain how the evidence undermines the argument.

Explanation

Question 2 begins with a simple statement of historiography—"some historians say..." You are then asked to provide evidence in support and opposition. Instead of three separate tasks, you are required to give two pieces of evidence in support, and one in opposition. In this example, the historical argument is probably something with which you are very familiar. Most European History teachers spend a bit of class time discussing this very question and all the evidence associated with it.

Part A can be completed with a brief discussion of some of the work accomplished during the middle ages. For instance, despite the reputed explosion of artistic achievement that marked the start of the Renaissance, medieval artists generated a great many works themselves. The Basilica San Marco in Venice is packed with pre-14th-century works and pre-Renaissance frescoes can be found in several old Italian churches, like San Clemente in Rome, and the abbey of San Gimignano.

For **Part B**, you might focus on the style change during the early Renaissance. Early works by Giotto, Masaccio, and Donatello showed the influence of humanism for the first time. These artists, rather than those of the middle ages, were the models for later Renaissance masters.

Although you still can't call the underwear on your head a hat and Goofy is still not exactly a dog, you might now begin to think of the Short-Answer Questions on the AP European History exam as writing exercises. You can probably see, from the two examples above, the ways in which you can apply your writing skills to earn full credit on the SAQ rubric. Fortunately for you, the Exercise Workbook for *Mastering the Essay* includes a full set of SAQ practice exercises. So practice away!

Appendix

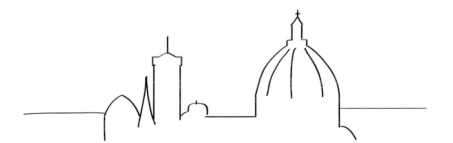

Key Terms

15th Century

Alighieri, Dante

Babylonian Captivity

Black Death

Buonarroti, Michelangelo

Castiglione, Baldassare

City-states

Conciliar Movement

Conversos

Florentine Academy

Frescos

Fuggers

Guilds

Holy Roman Emperor

Humanism

Hundred Years War

Inquisition

Machiavelli, Niccolò

Marranos

Michelangelo's David

Moriscos

Neoplatonism

Oration on the Dignity of Man

Papal States

Petrarch, Francesco

Pragmatic Sanction of the
  Bourges

Spice trade

Studia humanitatis

Peace of Lodi

War of the Roses

16th Century

Anabaptists

Anglican Church

Calvin, John

Colloquies

Commercial Revolution

Copernicus, Nicolas

Council of Trent

Edict of Nantes

English Reformation

Erasmus, Desiderius

Henry IV

Huguenots

Indulgences

Inquisition

Jesuits

Luther, Martin

More, Thomas

New Spain

Peace of Augsburg

Peace of Westphalia

Philip II

Poor Law

Predestination

Society of Jesus

Spanish Armada

Spanish Empire

Star Chamber

The Elect

The Ninety-Five Theses

The Prince

Thirty Years War

17th Century

Adolphus, Gustavus

Dissenters

Divine Right of Kings

English Civil War

Frederick William, the Great Elector

Galilei, Galileo

Geocentric

Habsburgs

Heliocentric

Holy Roman Empire

Kepler, Johannes

Levellers

Principia Mathematica

Richelieu, Cardinal

Romanovs

Scientific Revolution

The Starry Messenger

Time of Troubles

Period 2: 1648–1815

17th Century

Absolutism

Bacon, Francis

Colbert, Jean Baptiste

Commonwealth

Constitutional monarchy

Cromwell, Oliver

Descartes, René

Dialogue Concerning the Two Chief World Systems

Discourse on the Method

Fronde

Glorious Revolution

Historical and Critical Dictionary

Hobbes, Thomas

Intendent

Law Code of 1649

Locke, John

Louis XIV

Mercantilism

Natural Law

Natural Rights

Old Believers

Peter the Great

Prince Eugene of Savoy

Putting-out system

Razin, Stepan

Restoration

Second Treatise of Civil Government

Sobieski, John

Universal gravitation

Versailles

War of the League of Augsburg

18th Century

Agricultural Revolution

American Revolution

Ancien Régime

Arouet, Francois Marie (Voltaire)

August Decrees

A Vindication of the Rights of Woman

Bastille

Bourgeoisie

British East India Company

Burke, Edmund

Cahiers

Capture of the Bastille

Cardinal Fleury

Catherine the Great

Civil Constitution of the Clergy

Civil society

Committee of Public Safety

Conspiracy of Equals

Constitution of 1791

Cottage industry

Cotton gin

Declaration of Pillnitz

Declaration of the Rights of Man and Citizen

Diderot, Denis

Diplomatic Revolution

Directory

Enclosure Movement

Encyclopédie

Enlightened Despotism

Essay Concerning Human Understanding

Estate General

Flying shuttle

Frederick the Great

George III

Girondins

Great Fear

Hébertists

Invisible hand

Jacobins

Joseph II

Laborde, Jean-Joseph

Liberum Veto

Louis XV

Louis XVI

Maria Theresa

Mathematical Principles of Natural Philosophy

Middle Passage

Mississippi Bubble

Montagnards

Montesquieu, Baron De

National Assembly

National Convention

Newton, Sir Isaac

Partition of Poland

Treaty of Utrecht

Philosophes

Physiocrats

Pitt, Thomas

Pitt, William

Pragmatic Sanction of 1713

Pugachev's Rebellion

Robespierre, Maximilien

Rousseau, Jean-Jacques

Sans-culottes

Szlachta

Second Treatise of Government

Seven Years War

Silesia

Smith, Adam

South Sea Bubble

Spinning jenny

Spinoza, Baruch

Tabula rasa

Tennis Court Oath

The Spirit of the Laws

Thermidorian Reaction

Third Estate

Treaty of Campo-Formio

Treaty of Paris (1763)

Triangle of trade

United Kingdom of Britain

Walpole, Robert

War of the Austrian Succession

War of the Spanish Succession

Wealth of Nations

Wesley, John

Wilkes, John

19th Century

Act of Union 1801

Alexander I

Battle of Austerlitz

Battle of Trafalgar

Battle of Waterloo

Bonaparte, Napoleon

Concert of Europe

Concordat of 1801

Congress of Vienna

Consulate

Continental System

Fichte, Johann Gottlieb

Grand Army

Monroe Doctrine

Napoleonic Code

The Third of May, 1808

Period 3: 1815–1914

19th Century

Abdul Hamid II

Anarchism

Anti-Semitism

Atlantic Migration

Ausgleich

Austro-Prussian War

Battle of Sadowa

Berlin Conference of 1885

Bessemer process

Bismarck, Otto von

Blanc, Louis

Boer War

Bonaparte, Louis Napoleon

Boulanger Affair

Boxer Rebellion

Carbonari

Carlsbad Decrees

Cavour, Camillo di

Charles X

Chartism

Class consciousness

Classical liberalism

Communism

Communist Manifesto

Compromise of 1867

Congress of Aix-la-Chapelle

Congress of Berlin

Congress of Troppau

Conservatism

Corn Laws

Crimean War

Decembrist Revolt

Dreyfus Affair

Dual Monarchy

Eastern Question

Ems telegram

Eugenics

Fabian Society

Factory system

Fashoda Crisis

February Revolution of 1848

Fourier, Charles

Franco-Prussian War

Frankfurt Assembly

French Indochina

Freudian Psychology

Garibaldi, Giuseppe

Hegel, Friedrich

Herder, Johann Gottfried von

Indian Mutiny

Indian National Congress

Industrial Revolution

Industrial socialism

Internal combustion engine

International Congress of the Rights of Women

International Workingmen's Association

Irish Question

Iron law of wages

Jameson Raid

July Ordinances

July Revolution

Junkers

Kossuth, Louis

Kulturkampf

Laissez-faire

Liberalism

Lord Durham's Report

Manchester School

Mazzini, Giuseppe

Means of production

Meiji Restoration

Midlothian Campaign

National Union of Women's
  Suffrage Societies

National Workshops

Nationalism

New Imperialism

Nietzsche, Friedrich

Opium War

Origin of Species

Owen, Robert

Paris Commune

Peterloo Massacre

Philosophical Radicals

Positivism

Proletariat

Prussian Constitution of 1850

Ranke, Leopold von

Realpolitik

Reflections on Violence

Reform Bill of 1832

Reform Bill of 1867

Reform Bill of 1884

Revolutions of 1830

Revolutions of 1848

Rhodes, Cecil

Risorgimento

Romanticism

Russification

Russo-Turkish War of 1877–1878

Saint-Simon, Henri de

Schleswig-Holstein

Scientific socialism

Second Industrial Revolution

Sepoy Rebellion of 1857

Sino-Japanese War

Social Darwinism

Social Democrats

Steam engine

Stein, Baron Heinrich

Suez Canal

Syllabus of Errors

Taiping Rebellion

Tokugawa Rule

Treaty of Nanking

Treaty of Villafranca

Utopian socialism

Volksgeist

Watt, James

Young Turks

Ypsilanti, Alexander

Zollverein

20th Century

Balkan Crisis

Buchlau Agreement

Chinese Revolution

October Manifesto

Revolution of 1905

Russo-Japanese War

Sarajevo

Schlieffen Plan

Stolypin Reforms

Sun Yat-sen

Triple Alliance

Triple Entente

Period 4: 1914 – Present

20th Century

African Revolution

Andropov, Yuri V.

Anschluss

Apartheid

Appeasement

Aquino, Benigno

Arab-Israeli Wars

Atlantic Charter

Baruch Plan

Battle of Dien Bien Phu

Battle of the Somme

Battle of Tannenberg

Battle of Verdun

Berlin Airlift

Berlin Blockade

Berlin Wall

Blackshirts

Blum, Leon

Bolsheviks

Bretton Woods Conference

Brezhnev, Leonid

Cartel des Gauches

Castro, Fidel

Chernobyl

Chiang Kai-shek

Chinese Communism

Cold War

Collectivization

Commonwealth of Independent States

Communist Party

Containment

Corporate State

Council for Mutual Economic Assistance

Cuban Missile crisis

Cultural Revolution

De Klerk, F.W.

De Gaulle, Charles

Deng Xiaoping

Détente

Ecumenical Movement

Einstein, Albert

Eisenhower Doctrine

European Economic Community

Existentialism

Fascism

February/March Revolution

Fifth Republic (France)

Final Solution

First Battle of the Marne

First Battle of Ypres

Five-year plans

Fourteen Points

Fourth Republic (France)

Freikorps

French-Algerian War

Fundamentalism

Gandhi, Indira

Gandhi, Mohandas

General Agreement on Tariffs and Trade

Glasnost

Globalization

Good Neighbor Policy

Gorbachev, Mikhail

Great Depression

Great East Asia Co-Prosperity Sphere

Great Leap Forward

Green Revolution

Guernica

Guest Workers

Gulags

Helsinki Accords

Hungarian Revolution

India/Pakistan Independence

International Monetary Fund

Intifada

Iran-Iraq War

Irish Independence

Iron Curtain

Islamic Fundamentalism

John Paul II

Kemal, Mustafa

Khmer Rouge

Khrushchev, Nikita

Korean War

Lateran Agreement

Locarno Treaties

Maastricht Treaty

Maginot Line

Mao Zedong (Mao Tse-tung)

Marshall Plan

Marxist-Leninist

Mensheviks

Metropolis

Milosovich, Slobodan

Mitterrand, Francois

Monnet Plan

Munich Pact

National Socialist German
   Workers' Party

NATO

Nazi State

Nazi-Soviet Non-Aggression Pact

Nehru, Jawaharlal

New Economic Plan

Nonalignment

North Atlantic Treaty
   Organization

Nuclear arms race

Nuclear physics

Nuremberg Trials

October/November Revolution

Oil Embargo

Organization of American States

Organization of Petroleum
   Exporting Countries

Ostpolitik

Pact of Paris

Palestine Liberation Organization

Paris Peace Conference

Parliamentary socialism

Perestroika

Popular Front

Potsdam Conference

Prague Spring

Race to the Sea

Reunification of Germany

Revolutions of 1989

SALT I

SALT II

Second Vatican Council

Single Europe

Social Democrats

Solidarity

Soviet Constitution of 1923

Soviet Invasion of Afghanistan

Spanish Civil War

Spartacist Uprising

Sputnik

Star Wars (Strategic Defense Initiative)

START Talks

Statute of Westminster, 1931

Suez Crisis

Technocratic socialism

Teheran Conference

Thatcher, Margaret

The Wasteland

Theory of Relativity

Third International

Tiananmen Square Protests

Tito, Marshall

Totalitarianism

Treaty of Brest-Litovsk

Treaty of Rapallo

Treaty of Rome

Treaty of Versailles

Truman Doctrine

United Nations

V-2 rockets

Velvet Revolution

Vietnam War

Walesa, Lech

Warsaw Pact

Weimar Republic

Women's Liberation

Women's Social and Political Union

World Zionist Organization

Yalta Conference

Yeltsin, Boris

Youth Rebellion

Zionism

A Letter to Teachers

THE PURPOSE OF THIS BOOK is to help you teach advanced historical thinking and writing skills to your AP European History students. I hope that its design facilitates that purpose and, in the process, makes your job a bit easier.

As a history teacher, you are responsible for teaching centuries of content as well as an ever-growing list of skills—among them writing. The balance between content and skill-development has always been challenging for teachers in our discipline, especially for Advanced Placement teachers, and the newest AP Euro exam format has made our job even more complicated. We know that our students cannot face the new AP exam in May without a thorough understanding of historical concepts, nor can they succeed on the exam without practicing skills of analysis and written expression. This book was originally written to provide you with a resource for helping your students to hone their writing skills within the context of the AP Euro course content, and that mission is even more urgent since the College Board® has redesigned the exam.

Mastering the Essay guides students through a process for developing consistently strong thesis essays—the kind of writing necessary for the AP LEQ and DBQ, as well as most college-level essays. The process is simple and straightforward, and each unit of this book focuses on a key step in that process. The exercises accompanying each step are arranged chronologically within the Exercise Workbook so that you can quickly and easily address any step of the process at any point throughout the year.

Beyond this book, Sherpa Learning is providing *Mastering the Essay* users with a variety of additional online resources, offering flexibility to pick and choose content and to continually access new resources. Online you will find sample essays, scoring guidelines for each exercise, instructional resources for use in and out of the classroom, writing skills lessons that can be easily adapted to fit any historical unit, and an online forum for you to collaborate with other AP Euro teachers. Additionally, since Sherpa Learning believes educational publishing is a dynamic process, new resources are constantly being added, therefore users have access to a constant influx of new materials.

I hope that *Mastering the Essay* will become an integral part of your AP European History instructional plans, and that you and your students benefit from the skill lessons and practice exercises in this book. It has always been my goal to create a resource that works within today's classroom. If you should have comments or suggestions that might help to further this goal, please contact me directly at <u>Tony@MasteringTheEssay.com</u>.

Tony Maccarella
August 2017

Author's Acknowledgments

MASTERING THE ESSAY is the product of over 15 years of experience in the AP European History community. My many friends and colleagues at the annual AP Reading were indispensable in the creation and refinement of the *MTE* writing process, and many of them have continued to advise me throughout this Second Edition. Although there are still too many people to list them all, I would like to mention a few of the brightest stars in the AP European History constellation.

For their consistent encouragement about the book, teaching, and life in general, I am indebted to Carl Ackerman, Theresa Jesperson, Catherine Holden, Sharon Parker, and Bob O'Donnell. My good friends and former colleagues at Parsippany Hills, Steve Bechtler, Keith Campbell, and Robert Weinstein, were essential to the success of the First Edition and continued to "keep me in the game" as I worked through these revisions. Additionally, Kevin McCaffrey, Larry Treadwell, Matt Gutt, Jessica George, and Jerry Hurd, even after all these years, continue to spread the word about the value of the *MTE* writing process. I cannot thank them enough!

As in the past, I remain indebted to my publishers and friends, David Nazarian and Christine DeFranco at Sherpa Learning. Through their vision for Sherpa, David and Christine have helped me to create content of consistently high quality – a source of great pride.

Finally, again, I thank my family for their love and support. My mom and dad taught me the value of hard work, and Mom still never misses an opportunity to show off my books to her friends. My wife, Christine, continues to encourage me to keep writing, despite the odd hours; and my daughter, Mia, inspires me with her own passion and zest for life! None of it happens without them.

About the Author

TONY MACCARELLA, or as students past and present call him, "Mr. Mac," has been teaching social studies since 1982, and is currently teaching AP World History and AP Macroeconomics at Saddle River Day School, in Saddle River, NJ.

Prior to this, he taught AP European History at Parsippany Hills High School, in Parsippany, NJ for over 10 years. Additionally, Mr. Mac has taught AP U.S. History, Comparative Governments, Anthropology, Psychology, Microeconomics, and Military History.

Since 2002, Tony has served as a Reader and Table Leader for the AP European History exam for ETS. He is responsible for scoring AP European History exam questions, supervising other readers, and assisting with the clarification of scoring standards. You may also run into Tony at one of the many guest lecturer appearances he makes at social studies conference across the Northeast.

Tony is an avid traveler. He has bicycled across the United States, motorcycled to Sturgis and back, studied in China, and traveled throughout Italy with his wife, family, and students from seven different European History classes.